Book Two of
'He Heals the Broken Hearted' Trilogy:

Your Will Be Done

Beyond Powerlessness Fear-
Life Revealed in Love

Marina Carrier

Dedication

My Heavenly Mother, who rescued me from death many times and led me to the Heavenly Kingdom.

Acknowledgements

There are many people in the church who have walked with me or taught me, and I want to say Thank You to them. But there is a difference between standing with someone in their tears, praying for them and with them; and standing alongside a voice in the darkness which seeks to bring hope of God's love to many broken-hearted women and men. And Bishop Raphael is one of those, because he too seeks total trust in His Love.

And let me again thank Andrew Evans, a constant help, encourager, formatter, and provider of practical wisdom re the book, and all short-fall situations. Thanks to Martin, using hard-earned skills to help remove the creative tares from the text of my book; to Carl, editing the whole book into shape; thanks to Tatiana for providing a beautiful cover again; and Brian Skillen for renewed vision and help for broader publication of this book and the Trilogy.

I thank too those who encouraged me to persevere in this writing and allowed me space and time to work. So a special thank you to Diane, who kept the flat in order, and gave me of her wisdom and grace; to Andy and Liam who gave their time and work to do things I could no longer do when moving; and to my God-mother, and a nun-friend-sister, for their faithful love and prayers.

And thanks for that ground-swell of love that keeps me afloat in this life – to the Heavenly Saints who sustain me through prayer, and the Parish of St Andrews in Edinburgh,…to Paraskevi for our weekly calls, to RA for her faithfulness in checking up on Babushka (grandma!), to M and Fr M, and Fr Stephen -who share our journey, and those who message me on the phone –and to Chris and Sharon and the children giving me that human root of love that comes from family. Thank you all.

Preface

Dear Reader, When we talk about 'Your Will Be Done', as we do in the Lord's Prayer, it is so easy to say the Words without them landing anywhere!! But we are asking for God's Will to be done 'on earth, as in Heaven'. Thus we need to be prepared for these words to take root IN us and our lives, and to lift us to the Heavenly Kingdom. For those who have suffered trauma, and the dissociation and denial that it often leads to, it is not easy to accept the reality of God's love and Presence, at a rational level of the mind.

This book invites you to travel with Marina to serve in the depths and heights of Christ's love. We see the Grace she is given to enable her to serve in Love, in many different ways. But we will witness how this Grace, allows Light to penetrate further into the depths of trauma suffering. In accepting and owning the pain, loss and her sin of turning from God, she is further set free in Love, forgiveness and repentance.

So Dear Reader I want to invite you to speak from your self-protective 'rational' mind that maybe is unwilling to believe anything it cannot 'understand' – and say a prayer Marina has said for years,

'Lord I believe, help Thou my unbelief.'

May the Love of God and His Presence with you, and through you, become ever stronger, deeper and higher and bring you Joy and Love beyond the rational, in the Heavenly Kingdom of Fruitfulness and Grace…for Eternity,

Amen

Introduction

What is Powerlessness in the Context of 'Your Will Be Done'?

Imagine a journey dear reader, a journey of life. We are called to love God with all we are and our neighbour as ourselves -this IS the Will of God. However if we have not received early and pure human love, that will for good, for Love, is damaged. Not only do we not have a model of loving others, or God, we do not love ourselves in a life-giving way, nor have a will to push past difficulties. We have 'learned' to think of ourselves according to how we have been treated, and maybe to protect ourselves from more pain, which has often meant defeat or 'learned-helplessness' (the Encyclopaedia Britannica defines 'learned helplessness' as 'a mental state in which an organism forced to bear ….. stimuli that are painful or otherwise unpleasant, become unable or unwilling to avoid subsequent encounters with those stimuli, even if they are 'escapable', presumably because it had learned that it cannot control the situation.')

And fear of moving into the unknown holds us in a powerlessness position. We have a trauma mind rather than trust in the grace of God to do His Will through us. We have lost the will to say 'Yes' like Mary at least in areas unknown.

The Difficulties of Trauma 'Minds'

'Trauma Minds' and broken hearts* are part of the damage of those who have been abandoned, abused, neglected, and experienced physical, emotional, sexual or spiritual violence, particularly as children, even in utero. Their pure souls have suffered and in place of pure Love, have received hate, doubt, shame and evil which is against life and Love. Without immediate Loving and Pure input, they develop reactive behaviour both to on-going situations, and to developing relationships in the world in order to protect themselves from further pain.

It has been shown too that 'trauma' can affect genetic memory so there is potential for a generational effect...(-Professor Marcus Pembrey (UCL) presented a talk "Ghost in your genes: do human transgenerational responses contribute to developmental variation?" -March 2015- He referred to 'the Sins of the Fathers'.)

Healthy neural connections making the unity of body, soul and spirit are severed or distorted and the brain's capacities are literally 'damaged' by traumatic events.
Research (eg Stephen Poges [Polyvagal Theory]; Peter Levine [Resetting the Nervous System after Trauma]; Gabor Mate [5 levels of Compassion and Trauma Recovery]); has shown the effect on the vagus nerve (including auditory centres) and thus the working of the sympathetic and para-sympathetic nervous systems. These become prone to work normally, rather than exceptionally, in the 'fight and flight' mode, or worse still 'freeze' mode.
Only loving and none-stressful input and re-learning modifies, and eventually restores healthy functioning.**

(*The broken heart refers to the 'inner-being' when the neural connections of mind, emotions and will are divided and not working in harmony.)

But we need not despair, either for ourselves, or for others.
**Prayer is the most effective means of restoration!!
This is God's promise:

a people who walk in darkness, behold a great light; and you who dwell in the country of the shadow of death, upon you a light will shine.
(Isaiah 9:1b)

And whatever we have suffered as children or adults, the Lord promises: *'I will never leave or forsake you,'* so we may boldly say, with St Paul, (Hebrews 13:5-6):

The Lord is my helper;
I will not fear:
What can man do to me?'
(Psalm 117:6)

And indeed Isaiah promised that Christ would be the 'Wonderful Counsellor'. HOW TRUE!! (Isaiah 9:5)

Powerlessness, helplessness, and fear are thus facets of the traumatised reactions, particularly when children have been violently deterred from their conscious desire and effort to stop the external abuse.
Specifically, for children, or women, when 'authority' figures consistently abuse their power, failing to respect and honour the body, soul and spirit and right boundaries of the person, they are left in confusion. Their minds and hearts, no longer truly united, lose the ability to relate in love to their own needs, particularly when they are denied any respect, or free-will of choice and action.
Over time this trauma experience is covered up in some ways and goes into the subconscious, and new life grows. However the mini-deaths that occurred and the false beliefs that grew from them, need to be brought to Light to bring full redemption and liberation of Life. We need to have restoration with conscious response and choice of action, namely with a Will for God's Way in Love.

The Jabez prayer is a beautiful link between the traumatised mind full of 'pain', and the promises of God. Jabez, whose early life was 'full of pain' prays as a man….

'Lord bless me. Extend the boundaries of my territories, that You may be with me, that I cause no harm to anyone, and do not cause harm to myself.'
(1 Chronicles :(4:9-10)

And it is important to say, that these 'boundaries' can apply to any area of life where we sense limitation or blocks: – ways of thinking about something specific; perception of work or life opportunities; any understanding; at any level; the curses from others that affect false beliefs about who you are, or what you can do; and any 'territory' that does not conform to God's Love and purpose for your life. We need to remember that God is Creator of All Things – and the Redeemer – if we Seek, Knock and Ask. Glory to God in all things.

Awareness in my own Experience

When I was 'living for Christ' in work in Education I rarely felt 'blocked' – though I was frequently aware of 'waiting' for God to reveal the next step, or piece of information. I remember this happening when I needed to work with various Validation Bodies to create the new Modular Structure for the In-Service Courses in the Polytechnic. I was upheld and led and given vision of what was needed from Course Writing and Assessment Criteria for different level awards; to integrating all with Polytechnic Structures and wider-level Examination Boards and their criteria. And I was given grace to be in the right place at the right time.

And although I became aware of my defensiveness at times when needing to negotiate with others at Department level, I was enabled through courses I was sent on, to let go of that for 'a greater good'. I needed to lead other members of staff to engage in a more collaborative and sustainable system of courses for the serving teachers, but also to sustain and develop the staff involved.

But when this task was completed, I chose to move sideways to a Student Support role rather than apply for the permanent Head of Dept role..... However, the Polytechnic did not really see this as important and gave me very little time. I suddenly found myself with a timetable of school supervision, and hours of marking essays. My mind could no longer cope with all the rules, without love, ie support from the institution, and I didn't know how to pray.

When the lovelessness was reinforced through the 'no marriage' assertion of my partner, I found myself in tears of hopelessness. Truly I needed an extension of boundaries, that I did not understand, and did not know how to act!

Dear Reader, God Hears

God promises to hear
If we call to Him.
So that day, as
I owned my despair and hopelessness
In my tears, I heard my Name !
Deep within me I was encouraged.
Then day by day, I 'saw' things happening
For my good - beyond my action..
And I wanted to Thank this 'Thing'
Who was helping me and I started
Going to a church, finding -
My road back to my Heart of Faith.
Which lead to November 6th 1990
When I was invited to give my Life to Christ,
Through the God-fearing priest
Who heard God's prompting in his Heart.
Back home I drew an image of an open door
With Light flooding into the darkness.

God led me on this largely Inner Journey, now in a different church, but learning to surrender, and trust God's promptings and Voice. I was aware of a sense of powerlessness many times, particularly as my life in Christ led me to new paths and experiences. I remember being led to re-decorate the bedroom I had inherited in the house I had bought on my own. My new bedroom walls were covered in paper with small brown flowers, but the Lord was leading me to redecorate, and put-up particular rose patterned curtains with a matching bed-spread. It almost felt like death to take action, ie to take down the 'brown' (which resonated with the 'spiritual' colour of my childhood) in order to repaper and paint with a colour to match the curtains. In fact my son came to help me too – another gift.

It was a challenge to my soul to accept the love and beauty embodied in these small roses, and the re-decorating …when the little brown flowers were still serviceable!!!. (Until I gave my life to Christ, I had hated roses…and anything pink..). I needed to be open to receive God's Leading, Action and Love for me to enable this to happen – through me, and with help. All of these processes were simple, 'ordinary' acts that helped bring healing to the nervous system and my soul, because it was 'extending' my boundaries in terms of the 'good, beautiful and true'. This wallpaper example simply illustrates one of the multiple ways that God brings healing and change to our broken hearts and extends our trauma brains and Will for His Good! **Without these grounded changes there cannot be further growth in trust and love.**

And **Reader** this is for you too! Allow apparently unnecessary changes requiring ACTION to open up neural pathways in your body, mind and soul!! This illustrates again the connections of body and soul, soul and Spirit and emphasises the need for our 'Yes', our collaboration with God's work of restoration and redemption. (I'm sure many parents are finding healing when 'playing' with their children!)

Repetition of what we 'see the Father doing' brings healing and 'eyes to see'- enables 'extending boundaries', including wisdom to know when we need to put in a boundary to prevent further harm, and leads to Joy in Christ. Why do we experience 'Joy'? We experience Joy because we are acting by God's Spirit and 'Joy' is synonymous with 'being in Christ'. 'Let go and Let God!'

These new actions will include the opportunity to consciously accept and pray. It is important to accept the old feelings that emerge through bringing darkness to Light, but KNOW it is not the higher truth, and surrender it into Christ's Heart through prayer. He also knew pain and powerlessness on the Cross. He has been there. He will continue the work of healing and life-giving, if you are willing to invite Him into your depths, so ALL of you loves God – even unto death.

But Christ set an example for us. **He CHOSE to make it His will.** This is the secret of freedom within apparent loss. If we are willing, through God's Grace, to accept whatever was/is in our path, then the outcome and re-birth is in God's hands too.

You may want to turn your back on this, but choose the prayer, '*Lord I believe, help Thou my unbelief*'. God will not force anything; and although I have a tendency to jump off a cliff in wanting to do God's will, He has never taken me further than I can manage at any one time. **He helps me grow in understanding of the pain, loss and sin, and in my capacity to Love, with His Presence,** before He asks me to bear the burdens for others. The most hopeful prayer I can share with you is:
...'*Lord, I am willing, to be willing, to be willing...... to do your will*'.
In other words, I am turning from my position of rejection of God's Will, and I am giving Him my 'will' though at present it isn't conformed to 'Your's'...But I'm willing for it to happen.
This prayer has two major effects in terms of trauma brain. Firstly, it is very 'comforting' to have turned to God in honesty, and to have given Him your division and separation.
Secondly, there is an almost immediate 'softening' of the Heart, and tenderising of the mind.... because the Holy Spirit has been allowed in to the 'frozen' part of the mind and can start more healing. *'Not by might, not by power, but by My Spirit,' says the Lord.'*

Why is it so important to allow God into all your depths and powerlessness? God loves you, and while anything is hidden away – hiding in shame, or fear, bitterness or hatred, powerlessness, self-protection, or self-interest, He cannot love you fully because you are not open to receive that Love in some facet of yourself.

It may help to remember that we are called to be a Temple of the Holy Spirit. But if, like an iceberg, we only reveal one tenth of ourselves, we have much still hidden from view – which can cause damage to ourselves, and others. Always remember the prayer, 'Lord I believe, help Thou my unbelief.'

What is called into question is our 'will'... Jesus made it clear that we could not do this work of redemption on our own.

(The disciples asked, "Who then can be saved?" But Jesus looked at them and said, "*With man this is impossible, but with God all things are possible.*" – Matthew 19:25-26)

Neither can all this 'mess' become the most wonderful God-fearing and loving compost heap of Spiritual resources of joy, praise, mercy, truth, understanding and redemption, through your own efforts. This is not simply for yourself, but for all those that God wants to provide for through you. **God sent Christ into the world for this purpose!! And He needs you too! Together mankind and God, all will be well.**

God's Truth about Suffering

It is important to embrace the fact that the experiences that led you to a trauma mind and broken heart were never part of God's design but happened because 'man' followed his/her own desires and will. 'Evil' is the opposite of 'live' – and when evil has entered our lives, destroying behaviours and thinking enter our lives too. Christ came to set us free. Whoopee! And because we seek to be returned to our True selves, made in the Image of God (Genesis 1:26), and conformed to His Likeness, this redemption cannot be simply for ourselves.

YOU are the one, through Christ, who will have true understanding of the needs of sufferers AND knowledge of He who redeems. He needs our WILL – He needs our Yes……as Mary said that we may bear His Word and Spirit in our very being, deeper and deeper - as He brings healing. Gradually His Spirit of Truth overcomes the lies that have bound us to passivity and inaction through fear, denying our image IN HIM as a Child of God. (You may find 1 John Chapters 3 and 4 helpful and encouraging.)

It's all a process, day by day, of increasing faith, trust and willingness to be purified as we pray, surrender and open up our will to His Ways and purposes. If we hold on to the pain and suffering, and the old ways tied to 'evil' and self-protection, we cannot LIVE for the Living God in faith, hope and love. He allows discomfort and inaction to give us time to ponder and

surrender more to His direction and purposes.
We can ask for His help – if we seriously desire it – and He blesses us with Grace, and willingness to CHOOSE for His ways....so we become more and more conformed to His Likeness – leading to deification through the Holy Spirit (1 John 3:2).

Indeed, God's ways are not ours: Always He invites us lower in order to serve in greater Mystery!! We get to know our NOTHINGNESS and simply need to TRUST in His love, provision, and purposes, in Spirit and in Truth. We start to live more and more by Grace. And its important to stress the 'psychology' of Grace: it is the total trust in God's 'everythingness', and acceptance of our 'nothingness', in gratitude. And yet it is also acceptance that God wants to provide for others through us. We pray for help, and BELIEVE WE HAVE RECEIVED, AND ACT in love and service.

And this is the other side of what you have lived, dear soul. Apart from any pain and suffering and broken-ness you 'have', I KNOW that God has provided for you in your life already. I know that you have gifts and abilities- in His Spirit – which lifted you from the pit of your trauma suffering before you knew it. And He will do it again when your brokenness allows it and all ego and pride in 'knowing' are surrendered.

Welcome to this new phase of the journey – moving beyond the lies, so that you may live through your Divine Image and calling. Come Lord Jesus. Come Holy Spirit of Truth.

So after surrendering my life to Christ in the church, needing His Love to persevere, I was led to many new experiences. I was led to travel, lived in community, studied 'character' in Christ, did Bible study with the Holy Spirit (Old and New Testaments), and to serve people He led me to meet. After twenty plus years of learning under His Wing, He told me to *Face the Pain.* Because of all He had taught me I was enabled to listen to pains as He brought them to the Light. Deep, dark and originally soul-destroying- but now through the Cross and the Holy Spirit, Life-restoring. What is 'assumed' (owned) can be redeemed and increasingly integrated. His Healing brings us to wholeness, and holiness, as we know that only in Christ can we Live in Love. So He enabled me to own and confess my sin of running away from my pain, yet He never condemned me.

Thus, within Book 1 of this Trilogy, 'Treasures of Darkness: Facing Pain and finding Light' I arrived at a point knowing that God is Love **and loved me,** through Christ. He transforms all acknowledged pain, loss and destructive emotions and actions through repentance, surrender and blessing my enemies. Whatever the trials we pass through, whatever we suffered as children or in life, we can still find our peace and grace in Christ, through the Holy Spirit – always through His Spirit.

And this means turning to God in each moment, and choosing, and trusting in His ways of forgiveness, repentance and blessing. Repentance and turning to God becomes Life-giving (Ezekiel 18:23) and full of joy.

We saw how 'extending the boundaries' of the suffering-broken heart, through the Jabez* prayer, praise and obedience to His commandments are the only way to be built as a Temple of the Holy Spirit in closeness to the Holy Triune God. Passiveness and fear cease to be issues as we accept our life and purpose hidden in Christ, as a child of God, turned to God in prayer and praise, and above all TRUST. Glory to God alone. Welcome Life-giving Spirit. Welcome Word of Life.

**The Prayer of Jabez- 1 Chronicles 4:9-10*

Note to Readers – This book is focussed on the way God can use our circumstances to purify, heal and change us more into His Likeness when we are desiring to do His Will. **So the focus is on His work 'extending my boundaries' and revealing my need for prayer and humility, or change of understanding and behaviour. For this reason, other people and places are largely anonymised.**

Table of Contents

1

A New Look at the Powerlessness of Trauma in the Hands of God!!:

One night many years ago, when I was in the depths of my powerlessness and self-doubt, I woke with my mind in a whirlpool of thoughts! It felt like hell and I seemed to have no control over it. But the Holy Spirit was with me, though I knew it not, and I was led to draw this whirlpool. All I had as drawing implements were colour markers for the white board at the Polytechnic.

So I got some computer paper and started to scribble in blue..then found myself scribbling in red, then yellow, then black...... wow...so I saw different scribbles all overlaid. So I drew them again, separately; blue, in a neat spiral, then red, then yellow, and black. Then I drew a figure with arrows of blue, red, yellow and black attacking it. Each arrow was carrying a self-hating thought. Then I drew a yellow figure....and finally I heard the words in my mind, '*Don't think, ACT.*'

I guess I had taken '*every thought captive*'* (2 Cor.10:5). Glory to God. He was also showing that 'thinking' particularly 'over thinking' destroys LIFE!! He showed how the unredeemed muddled 'thinking' LED ME TO POWERLESSNESS – because in **fear** I was trying to work things out so I would not be attacked again. But in the Holy Spirit there is no fear because there is TOTAL trust in God and His Love, and blessing, forgiveness and repentance.

These self-hating thoughts stemmed from the trauma and abuse and the deeply rooted false beliefs that stem from it, at a psychological level. These are what prevent us from living freely for, and in, God's Spirit and our True Selves. Both our abuse as children, and subsequent oppression by authority figures is a denial of the grace, truth and righteous love given us to carry.
But the psychological effects of these denials of God's grace are significant - we certainly have some control, but we frequently control the wrong things - growth, change, love and our ability to freely give, receive and love!!! Our desire to control leads to passivity because it stems from fear.

We have lost whole-hearted trust in God, or authority, and our ability to hear our own boundaries and needs. I/We live in all sorts of denial, dissociation, and repression, and on the other hand, a desire to prove ourselves in order to overcome our shame at being alive. We are often living for false gods – false images of ourselves. For example, I was living for my image of myself as 'able to cope with anything' and making a god out of my 'intelligence'. We are all likely to make a 'god' out of the gift given to us!

We need the Holy Spirit and our spiritual Selves to lead us on, in, down- and up!! All the things God had given me in order to survive through my work became my identity, but they had also become burdens, and barriers to growth in relationship with God, myself, others, and God's purposes, which required true humility, love and obedience in Christ.

Dear Reader, does this feel familiar? Even though I had gone a long way in my walk with Christ, and had followed His path in many ways, still these issues would arise unbidden, and I needed to pray and remind myself of God's truth, and His love and purpose for me.

St Paisios talks prophetically about the effect of oppression on the human spirit making an unwillingness to take responsibility.... This is related to the effect of trauma.

'Nowadays we have been permeated by a spirit that one finds in communist countries. In Russia, even though they had an abundant crop (in 1990) there will be great hunger among the people. They did not harvest the grain on time; they went to the harvest in the autumn. But if the crop is not their own, how can they ache enough for it to go and harvest? Their life is a drudgery. They don't have the drive to go and create something because for so many years they were not free to create....so if it rains, they don't care.. But when the wheat is your own ... if it should rain, would you leave it to be lost? .....No, you'll lose your sleep in order to save it.' *P33/34 Spiritual Awakening, St Paisios of Mount*

Athos, Spiritual Counsels II, Sourati Monastery.

When we have reached the state of conscious acceptance of our trauma and loss – and at least desire, like St Paul, to see *'every loss as gain in knowing more of Christ'* (Phillipians 3:8)- then we are choosing to see God's 'action' and response, beyond the psychological reaction which tends to focus on defence from the world.

God tells us to *'Be Holy for I am holy'* (Leviticus 11:44) and thus we need to make a conscious decision (daily!) to choose for God's way. And as Christ tells us (John14:6) *'Jesus said to Thomas'* who has asked Jesus how they could know the way,

'I am the way, the truth, and the life. No one comes to the Father except through Me.'

It is important to repeat here that 'salvation' is not simply for an individual but in order that we can be witnesses,

'You are my witnesses," declares the LORD,
"and my servant whom I have chosen,
that you may know and believe me
and understand that I am he. (Isaiah 43:10)

In what way can we see God at work among us?

What is God's 'action' through the Holy Trinity that we might recognise in ourselves or others?

In **Christ at Prayer** we see Him going into the Desert after baptism, to prepare for His ministry through prayer and fasting; And see Him spending time alone seeking His Father's Heart after times of active service with the disciples.

In **Christ in the flesh** we see Christ obedient to the Father's timing – and then – teaching; serving through healing, blessing, 'tending the lambs and sheep' - always in LOVE; and doing what He saw the Father doing (eg His Mother's instructions to the

servants at the wedding, or those who came to Him;) or what the Father told Him to do;
and ultimately, He accepted total obedience to the Father.

And thus, in **Christ Crucified**: He was obedient to the Father unto death, yet even in His suffering showed mercy to the thief, and to His mother and St John. He left us His Words from the Cross to keep us on track when our worldly offerings in Him are refused:

> *Father forgive them they know not what they do; (Luke 23:34)*
> *Father - Into Your hands I commit my Spirit. (Luke 23:46)*

And in the **Work of the Holy Spirit** we experience God's Spiritual action:

Giving Life; purifying; clarifying; tenderising; healing; unifying; teaching; enlightening; uplifting; loving; providing wisdom; blessing; comforting; leading – when we ask, or need.

And we see **the Father's hand in Time:**
Providing; leading; causing; harmonising - in Time and Eternity.

I realise now how much my time in teaching was in God's hands… how much the Holy Spirit created my reasons and methods. The Lord continued to keep me focussed on God's ways in communicating new understanding to those who needed to learn and re-learn. As I taught children of all ages and abilities I realise the many ways I was enabled to open the learner to receive what they needed to learn. Eventually I found myself being led to enable (to build up in Christ) – not oppress - the teacher- learner (after the PhD when teaching teachers). The more it is important that the knowledge is put into practice, the more import is the enabling so it become functional 'knowing' truly expanding 'their boundaries' to bring new life and vision.

And I realise now that all God's teaching is to enable each one of us to grow in Grace, Truth, Love and desire to live for His Ways through His Spirit. In His Ways life is always integrated into the fullness of ourselves, so that it becomes blessing, a life-enhancing and liveable instruction for others, giving Him the glory. Anything outside this is of the world, the flesh or the devil and comes from man's brokenness, pride and or ego. And I guess I have lived out of all these at times, Lord have mercy..... But as lovers of God, vainglory or self-aggrandisement bring us neither peace nor love, nor do they serve the needs of others. We have to choose for the Holy Spirit of Truth and Love.

As we go forward into further awareness of 'Your Will be done' and beyond 'powerlessness', let's remember we are seeking to see God's Love and the realisation of His purposes. Yet **dear Reader**, I may have a commitment to His Will – in theory- but I want to remind you of 'fear', particularly of being abandoned, which early in my walk with Christ had reared its ugly head many times; and as you will see, still lay deep in my psyche. God needed to bring it to the Light to give me opportunity to allow Him to redeem it.

As I (we) allow His Grace to 'extend boundaries', old fears are challenged and thus we need to choose to release inappropriate fears of authority or situations. Most fear (apart from the fear - Awe -of God) is self-centred and lacking in faith

Dear Reader, one way God had gently melted 'fear' and passivity in the previous 20 years, was through the myriad ways of living for His Spirit which, in my 'seriousness' I had never dared acknowledge or give time to develop. I pray you may see some of the ways that you too have been encouraged to LIVE in life-giving creative ways, which you may not have seen as His Work. As we stay Present to His Spirit and surrender all need to Him – He enables Love to reign more fully, and we become conformed more and more to His Likeness.

Come with me, to acknowledge God's 'preparation' as I reflect on the journey when I was carried to learn more of 'life' in God's Love and purposes, so His ways could be 'life-bearing' for others.

2

Obedience – and Letting Go to let God Act

When writing up the time in the Hermitage in Wales, the Lord asked me to tell of the ways He had prepared me as He led me on the first 22 years with Him. That is, how did He provide to open my heart and mind to ways of being, or thinking, or skills that serve at a later stage for His purposes? I now offer a deeper and wider look at these blessings.

One of these was in relation to enabling learning. I was blessed as a teacher to have a great awareness of learning processes and the needs of learners, both intellectually but also in relation to so-called physical skills! I recall one 13 year old coming in to a badminton class and declaring she couldn't play badminton. I got the rest of the group started and sat her on the floor opposite me. We gradually built up the skills of seeing and receiving a rolling ball..then hitting it back with the hand..then throwing and catching and throwing back..then hitting it back by hand ..then with a table tennis bat. Eventually we graduated to standing and eventually to a badminton racket.

It was a joy to see this young woman receive joy in her heart as this skill and Self-control settled over the lies of 'I can't' and she realised she could!! But she'd needed to open the neural pathways and thinking skills that get programmed from childhood in some families, along with a change of mindset to say, 'I can'. It would have been fruitless to simply tell her - 'You can' without showing her **the Way**. There had to be 'action' both physically and neurologically. And because of God's work with my traumatised brain, I still have an ability to 'see' what pathways people need, in order to arrive at a new action, understanding, way of thinking/being, or how they need to shift from worldly thinking to God's ways and thought.

But God did this with me too and will do it with you if you keep the lies out of the way!! It's hard to grasp the dependence on Him I had as a writer. Despite many higher level studies and research, including a PhD, it was only after all these experiences, when I was writing up some research with teachers…I suddenly realised I could think a sentence in my head before I wrote it!!!! Normally

I would write (in Grace!) – then have to read it to sort it out!! So after giving my life to Christ in the Church, He led me to a writing course encouraging publication. I believe I did sell one or two articles but my soul was uncomfortable with this course, and though with my later Spiritual Father I suspect I would have completed it, I abandoned the course having earned the cost of it. I then started a Creative Writing course which truly opened areas that had never been touched. I realised I had very little sensory awareness and no sensory memories to call on. I had to start opening my mind and senses to blocked pathways and to creativity. Very healing. This course covered every facet of writing, including poetry. I was so grateful to God as there was no pressure to publish…just to grow and pray!

Much later on, I did a Journalism Writing Course because I wanted to be able to write succinctly. By then I had a Spiritual Father who insisted I complete the course even when the spirit of the course had shown itself to be very worldly. It helped me discern the spirit and purposes of writing…but it did enable me to write with Self control and find Life-giving subjects with human interest. Writing was further developed when I needed to combine poetry, prose and images in Calendars spreading the Word of God. But I go ahead of God!

When I was first brought back into the Church I returned to art in various forms, but many aspects were blocked by my 'trauma brain', and I had to be patient for God's timing. Colour did not feature in my awareness, nor much understanding of form, and I still lived out of shame at a deep level, so risking producing anything that could be 'seen' was almost painful and covered with shame and self-judging.

But as I had sat this teenage school-child down who could not 'play badminton' and DID relevant actions with her, so God did with me. I was prompted to start a 'Drawing in Colour Course' from the Open College of the Arts. I followed the lessons and received feedback from the tutor. It's hard for me to accept how 'backward' I was in seeing and understanding colour at that time!

It took me to the end of the course to even start to embrace and appreciate the seeing and mixing of colours that we learned. (I always said my childhood was just 'grey-brown'!)

Everything I did – I did through my head…not my eyes or heart!! But did God beat me up? No! When I followed His leading to Yorkshire, He provided me with one studio –leading me to get to know a precious child of His who became a dear friend. Then I was led to find a studio in Todmorden where I was living, where I could open the door to others to find and share the stillness of drawing and colour. That too touched needy souls. And this is important to note – whatever He offers – is always for a 'greater good'.

And God builds and does not tear down the broken-hearted, and thus this Drawing in Colour course eventually led to a year's Foundation Course in Edinburgh Leith School of Art when He called me to Scotland. In the beauty of the landscapes around – and with new eyes and heart, I was blessed to re-learn to see and appreciate, and to rejoice in God's creation. So at Leith I created the first calendar, 'Holy Island Reflections' 2001.

One year at a time, this led to making Calendars for 21 years!! He united body, soul and Spirit in this work providing for many people over the years as He opened my heart to 'see' and communicate His Word in landscapes, flowers or situations wherever I was. He enabled me to write from my opened heart what He was teaching, or to re-present, for example, the Prayers of St Paul.

Initially I needed to overcome – 'I can't, or I'm not worthy' when faced with a blank piece of paper and the invitation to create an image to the glory of God. I needed to choose to stand with the Truth - '*I can do all things through Christ who strengthens me.*' (Philippians 4:13) But then as I entered more into the mystery, there was contemplation and joy in seeing the Word before me in order to paint and communicate God's Love to others. The calendars were always initiated by the Holy Spirit who gave me themes directly

or through other people's requests. Sometimes, I really needed courage to trust I would be given time and grace, and faith that 'all will be well', in putting them together.
And there are other areas we need to overcome our 'passivity' as false expectations of ourselves, coming from trauma lead to either 'driven' or 'acting small' behaviours with others. Somehow these interpersonal relationships are locked in with self-protection, and with false notions of 'being a woman' or 'obedience' to God's commandments. Because of our false assumptions, our relationships with people have not always been 'mutual'. As a teacher I was given great love, and mutual respect, but outside that 'structured' relationship, I did not know how to accept and respect my own needs and boundaries. Let me give you an example.

On one occasion, I had taken a friend who had been in hospital, on holiday and was trying to be kind to her. This meant we'd spent the first two days going nowhere. We finally got out on the afternoon of the 3rd day.

We arrived to the South of Kintyre and I knew in my Spirit I must paint the rocks between the road and sea ...she went onto the sunny beach to draw. I sat on the concrete wall, and just reminded my Lord I was still in a body and I might need extra grace to forebear the hard seat! But as I drew and coloured the rocks with pastels - a poem was born at the same time – about the solidity of the rock despite the waves crashing on it – it was still secure in itself and held on to its own properties. Being formed within me was an awareness of His Presence in me and the need to hold on to His Grace and Truth. (I had been disturbed by the control of my friend's brokenness over the situation but hadn't know how to be 'kind' and not controlling of her.)

That night we discussed and agreed on another visit for the next day. The next day I was up early, taking my friend a cup-of tea at 8.30am and reminding her of what we had discussed the night before. I told her I would be leaving at 10.30am and if she wanted to come she would need to be ready. If she chose to stay at the

caravan I would see her when I returned. At 10.30 I left the caravan to go and get food from the fridge in the barn, and when I came back she was outside.
Not only did we have a mutually blessed day, but at the planned visit, a tannery at a beautiful castle in Kintyre, I was prompted to buy a £5 sheepskin pad. I thought it was for a new-born baby back in Edinburgh – until we later sat to paint and I found myself again sitting on concrete!! God is gentle and provides for our needs!! This is the God I have come to love, and to trust He loves and cares for my soul, body and Life in Him.

And because of this trust, I had agreed to spend the 9 months in Wales in the ex-cow-byre, listening to my pain. Out of the pain came revelations of His love, Life and Grace to overcome the deeper hidden darkness that was causing pain and heaviness within my soul. In this tiny place I had had to be largely still, without the 'satisfaction of action' apart from icon painting courses, building further on the art which He had initiated. I was surrendering more and more of my will, the previous gifts He had given and human ways of deciding what needed to be done. And thus my understanding of the pain aligned more and more with the suffering and redeeming work of Christ – 'At the Name of Jesus every knee shall bow'.

So in the 9 months of stillness I had tied all my pain, and growth to the work of redemption, purification, and acceptance of my life as a work of God, and for God. And now I was opened to His Work in leading me, in His Name, into service. This was whole-hearted, as far as I was able, but with the wonder of Christ's trust in the Father. Obedience in Love was my only desire whatever circumstances presented.

So now **(June 2013**), I was to move back to Edinburgh into my friend's house. She had been moved into a care home as she was no longer able to cope with either looking after herself or the different carers that came in to help her. I had been asked to serve as a sort of 'caretaker' of the empty house, organiser of the basic works, and being around to welcome the workmen for major works organised through the Power of Attorney (PofA). After the external stillness of the last 9 months while inner work was done, this was going to be very different.

Come with me, dear reader, into my first 'placement' after the time in the Hermitage allowing deeper transformation and purification of pain and grief. So with great readiness to serve I went forward in Christ's Love.

3

Staying Still in order to Live in Christ: Total trust in Surrender and Service:

Here I am, **dear Reader**, following Providential Care to a house in Edinburgh. It is in desperate need of clearing, cleansing and repair. I was given a task of continuing what I had undertaken some years before.

Now, as S has gone into a care home, the present P of A wanted a complete 'make-over' of the house so it could be let or sold to pay for her care beyond the immediate future. So I moved from Wales with minimal clothes etc, and spent a week at my son's in Grantown, then drove to Edinburgh before starting the initial tasks, including making a space I could live in.

Thursday 11th July

My heart is heavy
With the weight of love,
Overcoming in Christ's Name
The loss of life in my soul*.
Oh My Father in heaven
Uphold me this day
To sing with the sparrows
And rejoice in the stillness,
To Welcome the work
Of the day,
And fatigue of the body.
Help me to drink water
And eat what blesses –
I have no will for good.
Help me accept in You-
Denial of love
Denial of grace –
Loneliness
Covered by constant
Overcoming and prayer –
That no-one sees.
They know not what they do.

* In leaving the Hermitage I had lost that sense of 'integrity'.

Friday 12th July

Glory to God for the grace* with which He fills me..
Glory to God for the Light
Which reveals Truth
And brings it into Being.
Glory to God for our Oneness in Him –
Seeing division for what it is –
The lies of satan and sin.
Dear Lord Jesus have mercy on us.
One God, One Lord, One Spirit –
Amen, Amen, Amen.
Your Kingdom Come-
Your Will be done.

Apply for flats in Edinburgh (Council flats) in gentleness and truth. Pray for Unity of the Orthodox Church –

for Love
Harmony
And humility of the nations in My Word and Heart.

(**Comment** – Although I did not consciously act in disobedience, here is an invitation to a clear provision in Edinburgh beyond this work on S's house. If I had done what the Lord told me my path would have been 'full of grace' indeed, retaining (God -willing) an Edinburgh home-base beyond this labour of house reparation.)

But dear **Reader**, my trauma brain at that time could not believe that anything that coincided with my heart and desire, could possibly be acceptable!!! I pray for all those who need to have an open heart to receive Inner Promptings, confirmed by what others say!!

And thus July and August were committed to emptying, cleaning, repair of the cracked ceilings and walls, and painting the rooms that didn't need new floors.

July 23rd, 2013

My trust is in my Father and what He asks of me. I do not have any other sense than, **'Your will be done'**.

Oh, Beloved Lord may
Your Truth prevail over all
Sin and lies of darkness.
Come Holy Spirit
Come Lord of Joy, Love, Peace,
Come Lord of All.

Deep in the mystery of Your Presence
I sense fathomless Love, Peace, Joy.
Deep in Your Silence beyond Hope
Is Life Eternal in Grace.

Let us go Beloved
Into this day of time,
Given by God-
And carry His Love and Joy
To a hurting world.

Amen, my Joy, Amen.
Amen My child, Amen

I was involved in a lot of physical and logistical work – clearing and trying to wisely dispose of many books, papers and eventually the furniture.

> Time and again I would sense- 'too much'
> As more books demanded my mind to sift,
> Categorise and make sense of making
> Useful future for them. Then needing
> To follow through with delivering boxes,
> Piles to new homes, or charity shops.

More than once in this process I encountered spiritual 'defeat' which seemed to be in the house and the things I was needing to clear rather than in my 'head'. The following gives an example:

Wed. 24th July

'Yesterday emptied a box of papers and washed the cupboard in the sitting room! But a darkness came over me at one point and the defeat in this house inhabited me. Dear Lord give me courage to love and praise You, even in this darkness and defeat. Have mercy on me Lord for today. I need your grace and vision.'

Comment - Clearly S had suffered. I constantly needed to pray for grace to praise the Lord and persevere in love and faith. Fr Raphael had come and prayed a blessing on the house, the work and for the people involved, at the beginning of the process, and I often needed to recall his prayers and the sense of St Joseph praying for us.

Thursday 25th July

'.... I worship You –
I seek Your Face and Light…
(I heard 'reject' deep in my soul…)
Then: *Child you are not rejected by Me – I love you with an everlasting love – I provide for those I love. You will not paint today so be content – KNOW I AM with you.*
That's all child. Pray for love.

July 27th – Saturday

Jabez* – My Soul – Glory to God.

My Suffering Servant –
Be strengthened –
Be Encouraged –
Be enlivened by Grace,
Truth, Love and Joy –
Knowing you are in My Will.
Purpose- Hope- Gentleness
And Trust in the Father in ALL things –
At the Name of Jesus, every knee shall bow.

Everyday you 'suffer death and resurrection'
In order to serve more!
You have no Strength but Mine –
No desires in this life but My Will –
No love but my Love.
Have trust that I will provide.
The Holy Name will sustain you.

Yet God was also using this degradation of my mind with no human 'connectivity' for ongoing life or purpose, for greater healing as I needed to lean on Him and His Ways and He took me deeper.

(*Thus it seems that 'Jabez' refers to the part of me that suffered and is still in need of 'blessing and extension of boundaries' – according to the Jabez prayer.). I became increasingly aware that in order to be set free, I needed to OWN the pain hidden in my body, and free my mind from the 'reactions' through understanding, praise, thanksgiving and trust in God.

28th July Sunday

'I feel I am totally broken in my mind and cannot connect thoughts or sense except to communicate what God requires of me…And that seems to be 'Christ crucified'……

> *Child – Your mind was broken of all 'sense' by the action and effect of your step-father's behaviour.*
> *All connections, relationships, trust and sense of belonging or purpose were blown apart. You no longer believed in God, love or gentleness – all your female qualities were denied.* (I threew away all dolls, toys etc).
> *Through Me you have regained Love, but you long for wholeness in Christ.---- you long to make all things good – for God.*
> *Be patient for further healing and deliverance and know that I AM God – without Me you can do nothing. You are without grace IN ORDER to bring healing and wholeness to the broken—hearted. Habbakuk's faith in Me is your grace and virtue…..*

'Though nothing grows in the field….still I will trust in the God of my Salvation'. (see Habakkuk 3:17-19)*

Thursday August 1st

While praying:

While praying:

Darling of My Heart –
Have courage to overcome the darkness
Preventing you from painting icons……
Let Me work in you,
Let Me live in you without fear,
In total trust in the Father of all.
Let Me live in Love,
Gentleness and Justice.

Friday 2nd August

Justice is Mine – says the Lord.
Do not seek for yourself –
Let My Spirit work through you
In Love and Purity,
Righteousness and Truth.
Let My Hope, Grace
And Love- be your guide.
Let all that is within you
Praise His Holy Name.
Come Lord Jesus –
Holy One of God.'

Thus after some days of God encouraging me to do some iconography, finally on:

Friday 9th of August,

Light of Understanding Brings Release from Powerlessness

'Yesterday I fought the darkness of despair and will-lessness and determined to get on with the icon of St Martin.

As I listened to an Ancient Faith Radio broadcast, I realised that humanly (in my subconscious) hidden in this despair and powerlessness I had wanted to die. – This helped me understand my unwillingness to commit to anything. … but now responds to repentance, surrender to the Cross and praise for the death and resurrection of Christ!   Glory to God.

On Sunday 11th August

The Lord said:
Deep Peace belongs to the poor in Spirit –
Surrender all sense of injustice to the Cross –
Be willing to serve, bless and trust in
My Grace, Love and Blessing.

Gentleness will be your Strength,
Love will be your Truth,
Grace will be your Life and Energy.

Thank You for this Divine
Gift of Suffering –
That in You I overcome.

Dear Reader, One of the problems with our traumatised brain is that it tends to be all or nothing, and stuck in childish thinking. Despite the promptings of the Holy Spirit to paint and do something 'life GIVING' for my soul – it felt 'dangerous' and outside 'service'.

But one of the things we need to surrender to is God's love and provision. And that means accepting His love working through us in different ways. First of all, He will provide rest for the weary – and the work I was doing was very physical. We are asked in the Word to seek the 'Beautiful, noble and true' (Philippians 4:8) and painting icons and all it entails and the humility of giving up worldly ways, is indeed a surrender to His grace. So He was inviting me, us, to balance 'work and play', even when we are called to serve.

So, **dearest Reader** consider all these trials, which He enabled me to record, as insights into ways that He brings the dark to the Light in order to illustrate His invitations to lean on Him when seeking to do His Will. Book 3 will illustrate our essential Nature through Christ, as Children of God, who accept our Eternal Calling to Freedom through the Cross in Joy and Love.

By **August 15th** the plasterer had been redoing ceilings and repairing cracks in the wall. What a mess!

RH, PofA, and I had a meeting in B & Q store to finalise the new kitchen and bathroom fittings, after the surveyor had been to the house.
After one encounter with the plumbers when I was needing to explain an issue with the radiators, I realised truly 'God was with me'. Despite my stammer, I was enabled to explain what was needed. Glory to God.
Only in God could I continue in grace to face the daily clearing and cleaning of mess – outside – and within!!

Also on the **15th August** the garden clearance men came. They were to clear the back garden, bringing it all through the house. Everything living was being taken from the garden – including the magnolia tree. These were not my decisions but I had come to accept what IS and know that I couldn't do otherwise. (This matched the degradation of my soul as a child!!)– And **Dear Reader** – maybe yours too. But please do not be afraid. Once we own it and turn to God in trust, He will continue to gently lead us forward IN HIS STRENGTH to new awareness in Christ. After all, we are called to have no other thing than God, as God.)

We went on to prepare and start painting the front room downstairs, with A's help (a faithful helper from Church), and the back-room upstairs into which I would move when I returned from the trip to England and Wales with Hermitage contents.

With M's help we cleared and cleaned the attic to store S's paintings up there (**Friday 23rd August).**

Wednesday 28th August, I had been taking S to Mass to the RC Church near the Care Home and I took her this morning then went south, to see my friend J in Yorkshire to fulfil a promise to her.

She had sent me her draft book about 'The Long Return' of the exiled Jews, to read. I had promised I would give feedback but had had little time with the constant change at the house. I finished reading Thursday morning, and the rest of the day we spent discussing focus, purpose, 'golden links' as threads through the book etc. We finished about 6pm, knowing 'God is with us'.

Friday 30th August

I drove to my sister's and spent till Saturday helping her create some order– By the grace of God some order was restored, and black-bin bags filled the outside bin. (**PS 2023** – even my gifts of 'making order' were being shared!!)

ON the Sunday I drove to Swansea for Liturgy then to Llanybydder to clear the cottage and complete the move. But on Monday 2nd of September, I heard and wrote: *Child: touch nothing in the house, until the shed is made ready. Amen.*

Tuesday 3rd September

In 3 Fishermans' Row, Llanybydder Wales

Yesterday, as I prayed, I was given clear instructions through the Holy Spirit, to clear and empty the shed first *–then all will be easy.* The shed was prepared and packed in one day!

I was questioning the pain in my heart related to the fatigue of the work I was engaged in –

Facing the Darkness

Degradation and emptiness of my soul
And the pain of a loveless child –
Seeking always to be 'good enough to be loved.'
'Oh dear Lord only You can, and do,
Heal me that I can persevere
In You, without loss or pain.
Beloved I look to You to take
All self-interest from me -
That I rejoice I am alive in You
To the glory of the Father,
Through the Holy Spirit.
Come Holy Spirit'.
Child – Beloved of the Father,
Chosen by Him to bear His Name
And carry His Love into the world –
Be comforted that you share a little
Of the despising and rejection
Of our Lord and Saviour.
You are precious in God's sight.
Born to die- and Live again.

I went on in the journal, to reflect on questions about attitudes to women in the church, and about our (women's) salvation.
'As I come out of all forms of emotional and physical dissociation and denial of people's unloving behaviour, I feel the pain more,

and need to thank God for allowing me to suffer something of Christ's separation from You on the Cross… '

'The crown of thorns was not simply a physical but a mental agony.'
Father forgive them, they know not what they do.
"Weep not for me but weep for yourselves."

3am Monday 9th September.

(in a B&B near Walcott Hall ready for Icon Painting Course)

I want to witness to the wonder of the Cross and the glory of God in carrying me through the last 6 days of packing the cottage! There are more things for throwing away but the fact that all is packed is a miracle – and to God and the prayers of the saints be the glory. Truly if I do not stand in faith, I do not stand at all. Your grace IS sufficient for all my needs.

Beloved I adore You and thank You and praise You.

The next entry:

Wednesday September 18th in Edinburgh

The icon course (painting an icon of John the Baptist) made me aware of myself as a BEGINNER but yet by God's mercy the results give glory to God and St John. And as I was staying upstairs in the big Walcott house, 3 of us gathered for morning prayers for 3 of the mornings. A great Joy.

Then to Kinston and Liturgy of the Cross on Saturday 14th, and M and I drove to Llanybydder to pack the van (helped by my neighbour Tebor) – then back to Kinston.

Drove the van to Edinburgh on Monday 16th, and with A's help had it unpacked by 7.30pm. All the stuff in 2 rooms- waiting for flooring in other rooms and shed to be built and lined.

By **September 26th 2013**

The shed is up and lined and varnished and locks are on the doors. The floors are down in the 2 back rooms and I am in the upstairs back room. The bathroom is stripped out – the piping is done and yesterday Alan started on plastering the walls for tiling. The kitchen now has new hob, oven, sink and work top with splash backs – need minor fault repair.

I felt great weariness in my body – yet the grace of Christ enabled me to help M when he needed the shed ceiling cladding held in place. I persevered through the pain, then later realised this had been redeeming in some way as my stammer was back when I was trying to express something. The prayer of Jabez says, 'Lord extend my boundaries, that You may be with me….' – In ways I do not try to understand – if I am willing for the 'extension of my boundaries' physically then it leads to Light and Life and redemption in other areas!!

(Dear Reader – this is why part of our healing from trauma suffering is to allow our bodies to be used for work or service, thus releasing trauma memories locked in our bodies. Good Courage!

I was unable to express myself in 'truth' as a child. In fact, I have no memories of talking to anyone. I remember 'thinking' things, I remember my eyes filling with tears when my brother was teasing me, but I have no memory of talking before the age of 11.)

On Thursday 26th September

Summary of Entries –

I write about the advancement of the work on the shed, kitchen and bathroom – and reflect that my body is constantly weary. Sometimes I had help but I only write about the grace God was giving me to keep moving the work forward. Then:

'I am beginning to unpack some of (my) books and materials – but realised I could not put things in the shed as the roof still needed work. 'so, I must find 'work' balance by working in this room.'

'I pray for and intercede for Your little ones – I seek to find balance so I don't despair – but this house is made dirty every day and is still full of dis-order – all of which needs to be lifted – and BY YOUR GRACE AND MERCY - put in order.

Have mercy on me Lord.

Child of God be patient
Be Holy – be Loving
And Kind.
I will guide you with My Eye-
Comfort you with My Spirit –
Strengthen you in My Grace.
You are Mine –
And I, dear one of God,
Am yours.
Come Holy Spirit of Truth.

Friday 27th September

Seeking the Way…

I struggle to make myself pray
– yet I know He is with me.
Beloved Lord, Holy Father –
Your Will be done.
You went to the Cross for me.

You suffered in Your Body,
Soul, and Spirit – for me.
I ask for Your grace to
Overcome this defeat –
My desire for comfort,
Rest, strength of will and purpose.

I am walking on this path
And making this house beautiful,
Good and true- but again,
For those that come after!!

Lord I believe, help Thou my unbelief.
Dear Lord I confess my selfishness –
I thank You for Your love
For me and mankind.

Oh Jesus I believe You are
The Holy One of God –
I surrender to Your wisdom,
Mercy and Love.

Please help me that I may Live for You.
Let me carry my cross of abuse,
And 'self-abuse' and follow You.
Child – be still! What do you most desire?

To be pleasing to You and to Love You
With all my Heart, Mind and Soul,
And my neighbour as myself.

To Love Me is to love
what I have given you –
not simply working on
and restoring this house –
but painting – icons principally –
so start preparing the way.

Dear Reader: This intervention by God is fundamental in understanding the difficulties that traumatised souls have in accepting God's grace to provide for balance in their lives, when it does not appear to be overtly serving or giving (or by implication- pleasing) to others.

Like the other indications of God's encouragement to particular activity that I highlighted earlier – it was largely ignored. And not until this was being written up did I remember these words of God as INSTRUCTIONS of GOD!! Lord have mercy.

Tuesday 1st October

On the 29th September, I had been called to go to Chris (my son) in Grantown as he had been taken into hospital with chest-pain on Sunday am. In fact I was able to pick him up from hospital by 12.30am Monday as the blood tests showed no heart attack – I saw the children off to school then drove home to St Luke's (S's house).

On the following Sunday went to Dunblane on my own and saw that old wounds still hung over me, affecting my lack of trust in Spiritual/church life or the men who make it. O Lord have mercy.

Heavenly Father – all I want is a shed and space to work and pray – but my desire to serve takes me into the world –
And my prayer life leads me deeper into dark places and my weakness and need for You my God.

'Blessed Redeemer – I have no hope but in You. Make Your Will for me clear and shut all doors that are NOT of You.'

Sunday 6th October

Bruised by the shed not yet
Being complete (a shelter for my soul),
Yet I have persevered
In Your Strength and Grace
With the cross of this house.
I trust You, even as You reveal
My mother's secret hatred of me –
And the root of my self-hatred
And longing for her – and lack of bonding.
I forgive Lord, but You took me
For Yourself and fulfilled Your Word in me.
Please don't let the work of death
Destroy Your life in me-
Or overwhelm my Hope and Grace
And Your Truth.
P.S. And please guide me regarding a smaller car.

***LISTEN – in Your heart*:**

The Cross of dereliction -
Emptiness -
Feeling soul-less-
Father forgive them
They know not what they do.
Heart restored to wholeness by the wounds of Christ-
Love sanctified
Wounds redeemed (Pardoned)
Wholeness in Christ
Beauty in Love
Wisdom given to the loveless
Who seek to live by My Word,- not hatred.
Holiness belongs to the Life-giver.

He then gave me a list of house tasks to do!!!

Monday October 7th

I was urged to have courage to do what was needed in the house, and to pray for revelation of my calling in Christ. And to trust God with the shed, car, and my purse!!

Reflection following October 21st, 2013

Two major things happened following the above encounter with God, - though this list adds more details of blessings!

1) I had help to buy a 'new' car from a man who knew cars and had previously helped Fr A and others in the church to get a good car. I went to Glasgow to meet up with him – taking my old Fiat- and leaving it there.
2) Fr A encouraged me to go down south with him to the Certificate-giving as the Archbishop was coming. I had no intention of doing the Diploma course, but followed 'the Way' with Fr A. I wasinvited to join in with the Diploma students while waiting for the Archbishop. I was like a fish waiting to be caught, and by the end of the day was re-committed to following the Diploma course. (It embodied what I had hoped for from the Certificate Course.)
3) When I got back M had completed the ceiling of the shed, we got slabs laid around it, and I got shelves up so I could start to move painting stuff into the shed.
4) God ordered strict ordering of the house – throwing out or packing up more books and unwanted things – and God was saying here that I was to paint icons and write and essentially to 'live' in the house.

> The Priest from Kinston was also telling me to leave off the physical work 'and stay in my inner mountain'.

But in effect, I don't think I ever got a real 'vision' of living in that house as each task was delayed.....

I was needing to learn more of God's love in forbearing and forgiving as I experienced more darkness or disappointment – because people could not serve as they had promised. But my willingness to persevere and praise and give thanks, and LOVE grew, despite (or because of?) the personal deaths of my will and desire!!

Saturday 26th October 2013

Get up child and paint the rail in your room.
Be blessed with the task completed. I will uphold you.
Lord, I long to be creative and loving and true ….
*'Keep your mind in hell and do not despair…**

The morning arrives -
And at the same time
It waits for me
To receive it-
To say YES to it
And enter in
In the Name of Christ-
In Time and Eternity-
Making the morning
Alive in Christ.

And my hardened heart
Sees but does not feel
The wonder of this love –
As, hanging back,
She only feels the pain
Of the loveless nails
Of human loss.

Oh Beloved Lord
Have mercy on me-
You who made
The morning,
And gave and gives me life-
Let me say Yes
And not crucify You
Again – Your Will be done.
Amen, Amen.

*This is a direct quote from what God said to St Silouan when he was prevented from worshipping Christ because the devil got in the way. I had come to learn that the greatest sin was simply in not trusting God with the situation, however difficult.

The work on the house continued day by day, still clearing and ordering my room, and the living room downstairs, and A's occasional room.

Reflection from 2022

The Lord had always told me to keep listening to my heart, but I suspect, because I was ignoring my need to paint icons, I was running on empty, or at least only half-hearted. But I was able to get more help.

By **the end of October** I had enlisted more skilled help i.e., Alex, from church. I needed both his height and skill to paint the hallway upstairs and down the stair well – particularly the ceiling. S's birthday came and Aurora and I took her out for a birthday meal.

My Life in Christ' Spirit was being put to the test as people I had trusted were unable to fulfil what they said they could do. I had to be open to more 'patience'.:

All in the mystery of Love and Service.!! As He told me, I needed '*courage to stand and keep committing to MY LIFE.*'- accepting His LIFE in me through the Holy Spirit.

At the end of **November** I was crying out to the Lord but He pointed out that **I** (through my own will and mind) could not do His Work…*you can say Yes to My Spirit and TRUST.*

Monday 2nd December 2013

'Document your mind'
One day at a time –
Write your thoughts –
Hopes, desires, will, prayers,
And pray for fulfilment.

So I wrote Hopes, Desires, and Will and Prayers. – they are focussed on promises of God, or doing His will, are not worldly in the least but 'grounded' in His Love …and depend on the provision of God for time and place. God responded:

Child, the suffering servant is Mine –
You are Mine - Be encouraged
and Enlightened in all things.
You do not seek comfort –
But need rest and sleep
For recuperation of your mind
From long years of physical toil.
Be encouraged My beloved daughter.
Though you pass through the fire,
You will not be burned.
Though you pass through the waters,
They will not come over you.
You are Mine.

At the end of **November** I was inspired to start a calendar, and during these early days of December I was given time and grace, even in the night, to work on it. By **9th December** I am talking about printing it out – along with cards!!

But I reached exhaustion and the end of my tether when Alex had to withdraw from the painting work of the house because his wife's employers (in England) had also offered him a job. He had completed the ceilings above the stairs for which I was grateful, but I felt empty – without hope or vision. By that time, I was being physically sick if I did any gloss painting.

I went to Liturgy on **December 12th**, St Spyridon's Feast Day. I was empty of all hope or grace, but I knew I must come to this Liturgy! At the end of the Liturgy, I had vision of what needed to be done, I had heart to do what I could do, and I had confidence it would be done. Glory to God.

By the end of that day, the porch had been cleared and floors cleaned, with A's help, and the calendar was edited, and even 8 printed. I truly had 'eyes to see' that the downstairs hallway could be painted without stress (as only emulsion was needed) and the invitation to my granddaughters could stand for New Year.

As the Lord built me up to persevere, He was always encouraging me, to build up my 'neighbour' in love and faith and gentleness, through forgiving and calling on Him to provide the Love and Purity of Heart!

For example, I needed to build up those who were working in the house, not least to encourage them to give of their best. I found a simple cookbook in the house and learned how to make Borsch soup for lunch. The recipe was for a Russian Beetroot soup because I wanted to bless the Russian helper. However, I discovered one lunch time that Russian and Romanian Borsch soup are not the same. So, I had a disappointed Romanian – though he did enjoy getting fed for lunch, and with Grace received the soup in love!!

Prayer life

But as I prayed, and continued to listen each morning, He was also bringing to the Light the fact that deep in my soul I did not believe there was any point in 'taking His Love' or 'Sharing His Love' because no one believes me……

Comment: At this time I was still experiencing the pain of being 'despised and rejected' as a woman – and 'rational thinking' was arguing against the process of purification and growth of God's Love in my soul.

But every Act of Grace extends the boundaries of the soul through the Holy Spirit. And humanly there is 'loss' but we know Christ more. From my position in 2022, I have more trust in God to make a way – providing I keep persevering in prayer and obedience to His will!! **Dear Reader** – be open to the stepping-stones of faith, growth in Love, and Patient Perseverance in Love and Trust, and allow thc Holy Spirit to lead you.

22nd December

Glory to God Alone.

Women – in Christ –
Holy and pure of heart-
Entrusted with My Heart –
To love, forebear, bless, and
Minister in gentleness.
Blessed are you when men
Revile you and persecute you,
And say all manner of evil
Against you for My Sake –
For Yours is the Kingdom of Heaven.'….
Child- You will speak when spoken to and silence kings with My Word – My Wisdom – My Truth. Amen'.

My granddaughters came for New Year, which we shared with A and her son. They left on the **4th of January,** and I felt sadness! I needed to prepare work for the Diploma course, and also Janet from Todmorden came for a visit for a few days: then I left for the course at Kinston.

After the course:

I went to the Monastery– 14th -27th January

Always a blessing, greater purification,
And strengthening.
I told people about this saint
Who had helped me on December 12th!
(I couldn't remember his name!)
Then a stranger came to me
Saying she was prompted
To give me a wrist prayer rope-
From St Spyridon's monastery.
I was, and am, very touched
By this act of mercy and love.
Who can understand the mystery
Of our faith, and God's love,
Working through the Saints
And our hearts, which seek His Will!?
And still I turn to ask St Spyridon
When work needs doing
And I am empty of grace!!

Maybe this gift was some sort of 'material' proof' of God's love, because one aspect of the confession I had made at the Monastery to Fr B was my fear of being oppressed and subjugated without love – and my lack of trust in the Father's Heart or Provision.

This work continued to remind me of the need for the mind to surrender to the Will of God and be wholehearted with God.

Sunday 'I know the doubting Thomas in me is being changed and I understand better the mind-sets that stemmed from lack of faith or trust in God, or in man.'

Dear Reader – remember one of our trauma mindsets is 'dissociation'– feeling disconnected from yourself and the world around you and feeling uncertain about who you are. As a result we tend to isolate ourselves and seek control over events and

ourselves....without trust or love having access to the broken heart.
But in Christ all is changed – and after confession and Liturgy yesterday I was aware of my gratitude as the Eucharist brought life to what had been cut off from Life.

This morning I had to let more self control go, in order to face the death in my heart. I don't understand, but I have total trust in God to see this through. I sense I have to let go of all 'life' which Christ gave me – in order to gain life. If I don't do it, I am dead for always. Help me do it my God.

January 30th, 2014

Loving

I turn to You my Lord
And lift to You
The heart full of souls
Your Life has given-
Your compassion, grace
Forbearance and truth
My sufficiency.

Yet I sense You call me
On – in – up and
All I can do is give
You my hand
And follow You –
To green pastures.

In faith I continue,
In trust I seek Your Face,
In love I cry out to You-
Why have You abandoned me
Here on a cross?
But Your will be done.

Holy Soul be patient.
Adore Me, Praise Me,
Love Me – I am yours –
You are Mine.
Though you pass through waters-
They will not come over you;
Though you pass through fire
You will not be burned.

Reflection

2022 From this position and looking at this period in 2014 it is easy to see that God is still constantly trying to assure me of His Love, Presence, and His desire for my life in His. It is equally clear that through His Light shining into dark places as I pray, or need to seek His Grace to extend my boundaries of grace and mercy in action, there are things in the dark (i.e. in the subconscious) being brought to the Light.

What still surprises me, is how 'real' these feelings or experiences are in terms of 'threat' to Peace. But I guess this is the reason they could not be dealt with at the time of happening when there was no active faith and no means of articulating them or the conscious mind dealing with them. And yet in Christ, I now desire and will to accept each death as a 'gift' in knowing more of Christ.

So **dear Reader**, may you grasp hold of this clarity of thought, if you too are travelling the road of facing your pain and traumas and feel you are in chaos. Truly, accepting our suffering, with trust and prayer, praise and thanksgiving is the way through the pains and losses of our lives because we are allowing God to bring re-integration of soul and body, heart and mind. We cannot do it ourselves.

This is not done by some sweeping brush action – but day by day trusting that God is in charge and truly He will provide courage, wisdom, and Truth for each moment. The secret lies in praising God for every trial that brings these to the Light. In humility we CANNOT make 'rational' sense of our degradation, then or now; but like Christ forgive and look to God for resurrection and change.

Thursday 6th February 2014

I look to You dear Lord to overcome
This weariness.
Forgive me Lord that deep within
I want to die and come home to You.

Oh Father – I forgive the men of the church-
I forgive their intransigence
But they believe they are in Your unchangingness-
And that would make me wrong.
Come Holy Spirit of Truth.

In what way am I unchanging?
Unchanging Essence – I Am; I create; I Love; I provide; I shepherd; I redeem – Energies of God.

So I thank God for all the trials of this time asking of me more prayer for greater grace and patience; needing to get together all of S's paintings, making a guest list of S's old friends, and with the help of my granddaughters, and others from church, putting on an exhibition of S's paintings at the Craigmillar Community Arts Centre.

I was still getting flashbacks; and one time had a sense of a 'black-box' that needed listening to. But daily, I needed to simply praise to overcome the dread of life.

One day I confessed to God the difficulty I was having with one of priests at church and said: 'I cannot receive communion, till this is resolved.'

Child – Go in My Name to him – Confess your bitterness and fear of his tongue and interruptions to worship –and ***confess your lack of love for him in his pain.**** *Trust in My grace, mercy and truth – and put the outcome in My hands.*

PS I did – and came away weeping – unable to grasp my sins – except things I did not understand, and my disobedience to 'tradition'. (* **2023** Only now do I understand the Lord's words about the priest's 'pain'. I recently heard the priest had a condition that causes extreme pain at noise. Lord have mercy.)
Dear Reader, This underlines the fact, that if we make judgements, we are not being obedient to Christ. Only He knows the full picture.

By **March** I was beginning to consider that I would move to Kinston for the end of June – but meanwhile I was still completing the house; following up an invitation to contribute to an exhibition of paintings at Cockenzie House in East Lothian, with my own work; doing the course work for Kinston; praying Matins and Vespers during the week; and spending some time when prompted to listen to my inner being. It strengthened me when I did this:

March 15th

(I started praying in tongues…*)
Child - One God – One Lord – One Spirit-
One Voice. Have hope in
Your voice hidden in Me –
In Love, Truth and Grace.
You are Mine.
I will make you a fisher of men.
Believe, pray and rejoice
In your holy vision,
And trust in Me to provide.

Oh Mystery of Love
Awesome God – I understand
Nothing except Christ crucified,
And that sense of lovelessness
From the outside – and yet-
Unutterable grace to stand each day
With what comes within from You.
Jesus You are the Light of the World.
Show me the next step
Assignment
Icon drawing
Praying re 'Lost Soul'.

*'tongues' is a language given through the Holy Spirit which opens up communication with God. St Paul refers to it as 'one of the gifts of the Spirit' (1 Corinthians 12:4-6).

I was once praying in tongues with another Christian: he stopped; when my prayer was complete, I stopped; then we completed joint prayer in French- our shared language. He then said, 'I didn't know you spoke Hebrew.' 'I don't', I said. 'You were,' he replied. And he proceeded to tell me what I had said. So 'tongues' is not one language, but God provides according to His purposes, I guess. In that instant in Switzerland I had told God I would give back to Him all He had given me. In having been told what my Spirit was saying to God, I had some comfort when it happened, that this was in God's will.

Comment I do not habitually now pray in tongues, but only when moved by the Holy Spirit to reach out to God beyond my human knowing. It releases my spirit and re-connects me with God's Grace and Love. Maybe it not only enabled me to hear what God was saying to me on March 15th, but to continue in prayer for what He was asking of me.

Gathering of Entries

And the work on the house and garden continued to bring it closer to the vision RH, PofA, had for it. The garden had been top cleared with most of the elder bushes uprooted right at the beginning of the process, back in July/August, 2013 but the nettle roots needed a severe attack … by more than me!!

I arranged for two young men from church to come on the **23rd April…** but on my way to pick them up I saw a young man begging on Lothian Road, in Edinburgh. I said to the Lord, 'if he is still there as I come back, I will invite him for a day's work'. Having picked up T and Ag, I told them about this young man – and they were at peace with us inviting him.

The day was enveloped in the Love and Grace of God. Mm had some experience of gardening because his brother had had a gardening business, but he was not used to recent 'working hard'. Nor was he used to the friendship and respect he received as we tackled the horror and extent of the nettle roots. I forget what alcohol he had in his bottle, but every now and then he would feel the need to resort to its comfort, but he was also upheld by seeing the results of the hard work, by working with other young men on something life-giving and purposeful.

We all appreciated the coffee and lunch breaks to talk, rest and see what was happening. Mm kept commenting on how he was feeling and growing in hope for himself and his life! And as the black bags were being filled with nettle roots, we were gradually being able to rake the earth and re-create order to the garden where life giving plants could be seeded- (a very potent spiritual message for all of us!) Ag kept in touch with Mm for some years on Facebook.

I wrote this poem the day after the garden clearing:

Thursday 24th April

LOVE

LOVE embraced me/us yesterday
As with Mm, begging on Lothian Road,
Ag and T, from church,
We made order in the back garden.
Glory to God. And His Joy and Unity
Touched each one of us.

Gathering of Entries

The work on the garden continued as RH hired a contractor to lay a lawn and put down slabs across it to get to the shed, and I put in flowers round the edges of the lawn.

My journal entries were leading me deeper in and helping me accept what was coming next. But it was clear that sometimes, my anguish stemmed from emptying my soul to serve others that had not been 'of God', and yet I sensed intimacy with God through Christ.

Tuesday 29th April 2014

Silence

The Silence of God
Echoes in the darkness
And I cry to Him-
Give me Your Love-
Give me Your Life-
Give me Your Purpose
And do not leave me in this death -
Staggering in the dark-
Fighting demons that attack,
Or falling beneath their temptations.
Oh my God why have
You abandoned me?

My Lord and God
What am I not hearing/understanding
Seeing?
May I glorify You.

Child- stop prostituting yourself for others
-even good causes – and let My Voice,
Be your voice – My own One –
Let Me be/ dwell in your heart, mind, will
And forget not your promises to Me –
Your Father and your God.
Listen darling daughter and you will hear
Your promises from long ago….

Image – prostitute faithful to God.
Turned into a Queen of Beauty
Regal- royal – hearted – hoping
Pure – faithful – just - true
Loyal to GOD – loyal to His Holy servants
Radiant and bearing fruit.

Darling daughter, your prostitution pulls you from My Heart and Purpose - into your rational mind – even though you seek My Heart and Purpose. But do not be afraid. I will enable you to complete a Life of Columba in grace, truth and love – showing the mercy of God to repentant sinners.*

He opened up my understanding to 'see',
That when any of my 'hurts' are triggered
I am easily caught by an invitation to serve;
Because it provides satisfaction of my trauma
Mind and will triggered by unhealed hurts,
Rather than stay with the agony in my heart with Jesus.
That was why I had committed to writing
The St Columba Book for the Monastery.
But it no longer was the answer.
Yet in His mercy God did bless it –
Because I sought to let my Yes be Yes.
It was completed though it was never used anywhere!!

Gathering of Entries

Always God's response to my anguish, and awareness of my separation from His Heart, was patient guidance, and pointing me to simple ways in moving forward – to do what was needful, in praise and thanksgiving.

His Spirit led me to see dis-order as opportunity, and He showed me that the constant 'undertow' of –

'Why bother?– the church is made by men for men' was actually FEAR.

> – *Fear 'of raising your head above the parapet' Fear of justice and truth which leave you exposed to condemnation and anger of the prideful'.*

SO true!!! I needed more forgiveness and LOVE – for Perfect Love casts out all fear then 'courage' would be the fruit of being whole..

So I was continuing in fine tuning the order of the house, and garden; the work on the course including my visits to Kinston monthly. After another icon course at Walcott Hall, there was another visit to Kinston – but not for the course.

Sunday 18th May – At Kinston – when I had agreed to accept the room available in Church House – Kinston for the end of June.

Trepidation

.....

And now I must commit
To a new life in You-
Unknown and unseen
At present –
In the church
But committed to You
And Your Life.

Father forgive them
They know not what they do.

I have promised faithfulness to You
In the Orthodox church –
You dear Lord are the fulfiller
Of the Law of Righteousness in Love-
The fulfiller of mercy and salvation.

Child – be holy – obedient to the Holy Spirit.
True and without blaming, shaming or Self-compromise.
You are Mine. You will be tempted to despair
because you are Mine –
I will not allow you to be destroyed –
except for My sake.
Gentleness above all.

And at the end of May I went to the Monastery again.

Gathering of Entries

When I came to Switzerland in 1995/6 and finally had to re-learn French, I was also learning something of expressing my Heart, though I knew it not. God brought me into a closer relationship with Him in my Heart through French. As I grew in French and prayer, I discovered 'inner land' and an intimacy with God that I had never had in English. My English and 'learning' had developed in order to take me out of the pain in my heart, in order to live and provide me with a living. My mind was not able to help me overcome all the losses…until I had learned, through French, that I could have an intimate relationship with God in my Inner Being. 'J'appuis sur Toi Mon Dieu' (An inadequate translation is 'I hide in you My God')

At the Monastery (my first visit was 2007) my use of French helped my soul grow in relationships with God, people, the Sisters and visitors, and over the years the whole monastery, including the cemetery) was a harbour of God's Love for me. As a child I had had no language to express my pain, and I could not speak from my inner being, because I had believed I had to bear my own pain. LB (Fr J's wife) had been instrumental in enabling me to get beyond both denial, and dissociation in relation to the suffering and on-going effects in my life, over the last two years.

This visit was no exception and as I shared some of the despair and constant 'trouble in relation to eating and my jaw', she decided I needed some osteopathy, and made the appointment. This was for the day before I left. Deep calling to God, WITH DEEP TRUST in God I went with L for the appointment, and trusted God was doing a work that He would reveal in His own way.

(When I write in French I have
total trust and sense of Oneness…
But the English is so much more analytical.
In French I hear deep within,
I see God on High and I know
That only with His 'good-will,
Wisdom, Humour, Patience and Love'
I am prevented from falling.
In French I dwell in contemplation,
In English I am the servant!!
Lord have mercy.)

Dear Reader – Let us surrender all temptations to 'be something' – even left on the surface at the foot of the Cross- and let us call on the Holy Spirit to lead us in all things.

Wednesday 4th June (at the Monastery)

> 'When I work I put my trust in You,
> But when I am finished
> I am more empty
> And I need Holy Contemplation
> Of Your glory that I may live.

Gathering of Entries

Just as I have learned to TRUST in the efficacy of Prayer without immediate examination, so I trusted that the osteopathy on the jaw had a purpose of healing and re-alignment. With prayer, I still release tension from my jaw, but praise has brought me through the sense of anguish and pain & now I give thanks for every trial and any remaining memory or loss is indeed hidden in Christ in God.

And on the way back from the monastery I called in at Kinston and was shown the part-attic space I could use for iconography. Glory to God. Then back to Edinburgh and packing.

16th June – Edinburgh

Reconciliation

Man and God-
One in Divine Grace-
Man and woman
One in Divine purpose-
Body and Soul
United in Divine Action
And Praising God
And doing His will –
One step at a time.
I adore You my Lord and my God.
Your will be done
Your hope, vision, truth.

Darling child, be enamoured by My Love -
-Let Me strengthen you with My Love in every dimension.
Pray, trust, act. I will provide for all your needs. Holy Hope.

22nd June

Believe and trust that I love you-
In all things give thanks – in all things praise,
-in all things seek My Heart, Mind and Will
In each step.
Praise, Praise, Praise, Praise God –
Father, Son and Holy Spirit.

Summary of events leading to departure.

The days following this were taken up with packing, throwing away, organising the van and clearing the house. There were a whole team of people who provided willing hands preparing essential furniture, and book-binding, iconography, and computer & office essentials that needed to go. There were also books packed in bags, which M packed between pieces of furniture on the day of departure.

Just inside the back door of the van were plants I had kept alive in pots during the stripping of the garden.

And the house and garden were left fit to rent or sell as RH, PofA, saw fit. The task I had committed to was complete. Glory to God for all the hands and hearts who had brought it about.

June 29th, 2014

By God's grace I drove the van down to Kinston. I have little memory of that drive, which means I was carried by God's grace. I have a memory of being in front of Church House with the back of the van open, trusting in faith, 'All will be well'. Glory to God.

4

Staying Still, in Order to Live in Christ: In Obedience in the Church

June 2014

I have a memory of being in front of Church House with the back of the van open. Glory to God I had arrived safely.

I was not alone on the driveway. The priest and three young men who lived in the house were there too. Much stuff to unload it seemed, yet gifts God had given lay within it. I was there to stay; and was asked to empty the van and tell the helpers where each thing was to go. God gave me grace to do what was asked; and God's provisions were guided to my cell, the communal kitchen, or the attic.

Unfortunately, the bags of books had to be removed first at each 'layer' of the van in order to release the furniture. I was putting my right arm's strength to the test lifting bags of books at arm's length from behind bookcases etc. About half way through the emptying, as tears were pouring down my face, I knew I had damaged my right arm/shoulder, and courage, through the pain, was enabling me to persevere. (I had no sense that an option was to ask for help.*) By God's grace, I completed the task of emptying the van – and the helpers had dispersed the bags and furniture to the appropriate spaces.

The experience of physical pain was a witness to the aspect of Christ's suffering that I had always run away from…both in terms of memories, but also a part of the Cross I did not want. I learned that day that 'even there God is with us'.

For the rest of the day, I sought to start creating order out of the apparent chaos of unpacked and unordered boxes and furniture. I was blessed to recognise my human needs!! I knew I needed to make up my 'box bed' in my cell; enable my eating utensils and food to find a place in the kitchen – at least for the time being; and start to see how I might make the upstairs attic space into a useable icon studio. One step at a time in God's grace.

*__Dear Reader__, we need to recognise this pattern of behaviour as being rooted in the powerlessness of abuse. Please learn from this. And know that this is not God's Way. If you are in a situation where your strength is really being stretched unmercifully – ask for help. You might not get it, but you have accepted your need for divine help and maybe the angels will help early enough to prevent actual damage.

I am reminded of a story about some of St Columba's monks who had been 'borrowed' by another Abbot to help with building a monastery. St Columba became spiritually aware one day that his monks were suffering under the harsh regime of this other Abbot…and he began to pray for them. The Holy Spirit convicted the Abbot of his harshness towards these monks – and he ordered rest and food. He then changed the regime, showing them kindness and balance so they could willingly and lovingly give their service. This is God's way.

Monday 30th June

Overcoming

Bringing life into the hardened heart,
Feeling once more the pain and loss-
And knowing now – only You can save-
Lord Jesus Christ have mercy on us.
Give us courage to overcome
The lies of satan that say there is no hope-
No God to make a difference-
Oh Beloved Lord what a lie –
You, waiting to give us NEW LIFE
In Hope, Love and Service.
Lord have mercy.
I love You Lord.
I love you child.
Walking into the Light –
I will lead you by Grace
Both to will and do My Will.
You are not to be anxious
But trust, praise and love.
You are Mine, and I AM yours.
Gentleness and Truth bound in union. Amen, Amen, Amen

4th July

Sustain me Lord in righteousness
And prayer for this nation.
Help me accept to just 'pray'
Without having a sense of
Your Presence, Grace, Truth.

Child- you are Mine,
your only comfort is in Me,
your only strength is in Me.
Your prayer comes from My Holy Spirit –
It is no prayer that is not from a whole heart.

Monday 7th July

The Hole

Even here You promise to be with me-
I seek Your Face in this darkness-
Though I know You are carrying me
In this despair and sickness.
I have tried to overcome
To find the Beautiful, Good and True
Within -But I cannot fight evil alone –
And even You had to die on the Cross –
Allowing evil and death to defeat Your humanity.
So - yet I will praise You and trust You.

Deep within I want to run away
And find life, but this would
Move with me – I cannot hide
From this unmet need –
This cause of death
This broken body and life.
Oh my God have mercy on me.

Brokenness, loss, forgiveness
Allowing me to see and experience
The death on the Cross –
Yet no loss – God is with us –
And to Him be all glory and honour.

Trust daughter....
Trust Me to guide you – and the saints to pray for you.

Forgive your mother for her lovelessness...

Gathering of Entries

Since moving in, and up to 10th of July, the Priest and his wife have given me help to get shelves up in the attic space which will be used for iconography. (I have brought work surfaces and storage desk from S's.) Also more shelf space has gone up in the small cell (approx. 6'x9' + door opening space.). This space functions as my bedroom, sitting room, office/computer space plus storage and drawer space for clothes. It also has floor space for Beauty's bed! Glory to God all my spaces are 'worked together for good-enough' prior to leaving to go back north to Edinburgh, and then to the Monastery.

Comment from 2022/3

I have little memory of these first days and no sense of anything but being in God's will. Slowly my being was becoming 'in' this place. Ready to be 'still' but first I had committed to going again to the monastery.

Thursday 10th July. (Leaving today to go to Todmorden, then Edinburgh, then on Monday to the Monastery – and feeling despair at more packing.!)

Allow Me to write

Overcoming all darkness – despair
Fear, shortcoming –
Holy Trust in the Eternal Grace
Of God the Almighty Father -
Through the Incarnation –
Will always bring Peace,
Love, Joy.
These are not sentiments –
Not human constructs
But statements of Being in God.-
Given in God, by God, for God.
Let Me win my darling daughter.

Oh my Beloved Lord
To You be all glory, honour and power.
Forgive me and forgive me for being anxious.
You are the overcoming One.
I adore You – I love You – I honour You.
I will write from now on
To enable you to bring all to the Light.
Do not be afraid.
What is assumed, can be redeemed.*

Redeeming the cross
By Grace and Truth
Love and Compassion.
you held by Me -
We holding others.

*Whatever separation from God we accept/confess – i.e. 'assume' take as 'ours' but confess our powerlessness to change this on our own, we are placing our need in God's hands – and through Christ it can be redeemed.

This, here is your place of Resurrection. Do not be afraid.

(Yes I believe and trust in Jesus Christ the Holy One of God – Saviour of the world.)

Do not be afraid.

Comment It was true that this place held no human attraction for me. Apart from Jay in a nearby town, I knew no-one to whom I could turn as friend or family. I was truly standing in Christ, in God. And in Christ I needed to turn in faith always to His Trust in the Father's Love and provision. Lord have mercy.

Yet I brought with me the Grace of the Gifts God had given me, including DIYskills, bookbinding, iconography (though at early development), computer/writing skills, and willingness to respond to need.

14th July 2014 In the Monastery

Now in the Monastery with RA who I met up with again in Edinburgh – and I've now left S's house for the last time.

I am struggling with physical and spiritual demands and expectations. Lord have mercy.

Lord give me discipline and strength to overcome my half-heartedness.

(The following shows some answered prayer re: this last entry)

Tuesday 15th July

Beloved of My Heart
Why do you not trust
My Grace alive in you?
Lord I am afraid of my confidence
In case it is false-
Or crushes the broken and lost.
How do I live through You
except in gentleness?
Child – dearest one
Gentleness is full of Holy Strength
Without self or worldly power
But full of Grace and Truth.

Lord, I WANT to live for You
In You, by You
But it seems my mind
Gets in the way – says it does not know
What to do that is kind and loving –
So chooses to play a game…
Oh Lord, have mercy on me.
I have to trust my God
In You and Your provision.

In the monastery I followed the pattern of services, but above all rejoiced to see well-loved sisters and mothers, and enjoyed the gardens and walks around the monastery.

Saturday 19th July

In the Church at the Monastery.

I am by St Seraphim's icon– to listen and surrender to God.

Child- Love your neighbour as yourself: that means to submit as if to Christ – and leave the outcome to God the Father – Trust in God in all things. *

Forgive me Lord – I hate being dominated – Oh dear Lord forgive me for my pride.

Forgive yourself and let the Cross be your guide.

Amen Lord- I am willing.

Let the Holy Spirit uphold you at EVERY moment – in working, waking, walking. I love you and pray for you to overcome every trial and temptation to self-protection.

Blessed St Seraphim, thank you.

That is all. God be with you.

*At one time in the past I had had this understanding, and instead of hurrying up the friend I had taken to a café for a cup of tea, I handed my needs back to God and prayed.

Almost immediately she said, 'Come on Marina, you've got to get back to Nailsea for your meeting. We ought to go'!! I was so grateful to God and to my friend who witnessed to Christ within her.

Sunday 20th July 2014

Still at the Monastery

(Comment- I love the Way God prepares us and provides what we need to confirm His purposes and ways.)

<u>Sunday afternoon Talk in the Monastery Library</u> **(Fr J?)**
(Quotes from notes taken)

Q What do people most need to hear?'

A. All that unites us in Christ.

'The aim of our life is to build us in Christ – that all we do is in Christ and therefore united with one another (and living for God's purpose).

'Why are we born into this world of paradox? – To join us to the Kingdom of Heavenly Love. Without Christ and the STAR to guide us we would be broken on the rocks by the waves of life.

'Our life in the Church starts with our relationship with Christ, and through Him with the Father and the Holy Spirit. All relationships depend on Love in all our life. – What we DO is witness to our life in Christ.

Q How do we build this relationship with Christ?

1. **<u>Hear</u> the Word of God – the Gospels; Epistles; Psalms and the words of the saints.**
   With the Word we learn how to address our prayers to God: so many in the Bible, including Christ have prayed to the Father in different circumstances…

2. **Do the Word of God** - Listening also means 'obedience' – and it's not those who 'hear' the Word of God but those who put it into practice – those who live the practice of the Good News (1 John 5:1-3). Christ is hidden in the commandments because Christ tells us that if we seek to put His Word into practise, He and the Father will come and live with us.

3. **Prayer**

   Psalm 46: 'Be still (silent) and know that I am God'. And **LISTEN.**

   No one can 'listen' if they are not silent and keeping still. It's important to chase the 'old-man' (the unredeemed self, Romans 6:6) and find the regenerated thought of Christ.

   We are thus changing the thoughts and nature of our 'dialogue' within- learning to discern whether we are speaking with ourself or a demon. 'At the Name of Jesus every knee will bow. ' (Philippians 2:10)

   Each soul must find the path of personal prayer with, and to, Jesus.

   Gradually through Christ we enter more and more into life in Christ.

4. **Sacraments – Salvation through the Church**

   All the Mysteries of the church are given to find union with Christ…but both confession and the Eucharist have to be received with humble, contrite hearts, according to God's Word. Nothing is impossible for God (Genesis 18:14, Jeremiah 32:17), but we need to be willing to be willing to live for His Will and purposes. The Mysteries are not simply 'things you do', but acts of open-ness to union with God.

No degree of sin or death is a barrier for God if we are willing to be open to His Life, Love and Purity of Heart. All that is bad is chased by the Blessed Body and Blood – and sitting at the feet of Christ. We receive nothing but God Himself by self-emptying in love and humility.

5. **Humility and Love of Our Neighbour**

   Fraternal love is important – Christ was humble in His humanity – We need to honour our neighbours as bearers of the image of Christ as we allow His image to reign in us in love and gentleness.

   St Silouan said, 'If all sought the humility of Christ, the world would change'.

Above all else the attitude to others shows the state of the soul.'

PS. What a blessing this teaching was to carry me back to the Parish.

Wednesday 23rd July

1st Day in my cell in Kinston

'Out of the depths I have cried to You – hear me oh Lord.'
(Psalm 130:1-2)

My Beloved, I trust in You to help me overcome the disorder of the room – that it may glorify You and be a witness to Your Grace and Work through me. Come Lord Jesus.

A Remembered Prayer

Dear Reader – As you journey with me in this service, I want you to remember God's purposes! Some years ago, I had said to God I didn't mind what I suffered in this life, if I could go to be with Him for Eternal Life. So, the Holy Spirit at work in me knows this, my broken heart/mind does not always remember. But every sense of lovelessness, is, in Heavenly Truth, an invitation to redeem the lovelessness in me and my history, through prayer, forgiveness and praise. And then to turn it into prayer for others. This is why St Peter says, *'Count every trial as blessing.'* Remember we aim to be filled with the Holy Spirit and become a Temple for His Life, obedient to God the Father.
I'm inviting you to see everything that happens as GIFT of God (beyond understanding) and answer to the prayer I made and the surrender of all human will to His Will in the service He chooses for me. Remember the two prayers that we need to hang on to, 'Lord I believe, help Thou my unbelief', and 'Lord I am willing, to be willing. (x?)………to do Your will.' In other words, instead of having our back to the Lord, we face Him but acknowledge we yet need help!!

Monday 28th July

'I will not rest till your salvation shines out like a light'
Darling of My Heart – You are Precious to Me -
I love you – more than you can conceive –
You are Precious in My sight and
I make a way for you that at present
You do not see. Do not be afraid at
Your apparent intransigence and
Powerlessness with little Self-control.
I Am with you – I will overcome.
Forgive your mother for not wanting you
Or caring for you and thank Me
For all the overcoming and upholding
I gave you and her – Yes – and all the broken and lost.

Now darling daughter –
Thank you for the prayers –
Get up and go and let the dog out,
Eat fruit for breakfast,
Then go and work in the icon painting room.
I love you and will provide.

Sunday 10th August

Weeping

Lord You tell the women to weep
For themselves – not You.
I weep Lord, whether for You or myself
I no longer know.

I surrendered my half hidden memory
Of 'the cross' to You, before the
Eucharist, and now the pain of loss,
Degradation, isolation and
Alienation is almost unbearable-
With the sense that God has left me
Without comfort or hope—

But before the Eucharist I heard,
That at Your death – Your soul went
To hell to save souls –
And Your body to the grave -
And rose uncorrupted.

So my hope is in You –
For Life Eternal beyond
This death.

I had wondered about going out-
To take Beauty and to discover
A new reserve or place to be with God.
But before Liturgy I went to the top room
And tidied and prepared it for work.

Oh My God, do not abandon me
To unrighteousness or running away.
Show me the way to go.

Child- I am with you in your pain and loss-
Do NOT go out – you would be running away-
Go and paint your Holy Mother Icon.
This is My Heart for you today.-
Take Beauty out into the garden
And lock the Church.
Then go upstairs and leave her
In your room. You are Mine,

Sunday 17th August 2014

(after a struggle with conflicting thoughts, oughts and finally seeking God's Spirit's leading…..

Do not go today, I need you here..)

Faith, Hope and Love
In the Holy Spirit,
Bring Peace and Hope,
Perseverance and Joy
In all things –
Trusting in the Father
Through the Holy Spirit
In Christ Jesus. Amen.

Later-

Heulwen Marina Carrier

At the Name of Jesus every knee shall bow.

PRIDE -
Overcoming death in Christ
All gifts have to be surrendered
To God's purpose and the salvation of souls.
Humility – even unto death

God's Word:

Throughout the journaling of the last 24 years, God has led me by His Word. Now my desires for Christ are in the context of living for Christ, His Word and Spirit within an actual church context. I am called to be 'still' and obedient within this situation, while still aware of unhealed human hurts in my soul and body. These hurts seem to be triggered by any experience of

indifference, or comparison with others. I turn this to Christ…my Life and hope are in Him. Thank You Lord for every apparent trial.
And I know beyond 'knowing' that desires that stem from the broken heart are likely to be self-seeking. I pray for His Love, Spirit and Grace to act in purity and to bind all in Love, forbearance and patience.

I know that only my Lord's Grace and the Holy Spirit can do this. Prayer at all time keeps me still and listening, knowing that I could not do this alone.

Yet, DEAR READER, I was to learn the inordinate mercy of God for my soul and life, and YOURS, as He promises to be our Strength, and all we need in His service.

August 19th 2014

Oh Beloved Lord, have mercy on me
Keep me in purity and love.
How do I overcome my neediness
While serving others?
Oh my God have mercy on me.

You are without stain-
Forgive those who abandoned you
To darkness and sin-
Forgive your own despair and lovelessness-
Forgive your mother's sin and intransigence.

I will provide and overcome – I will be your Strength – righteousness – love and truth. I will be your God – and you MY servant, friend -
And guide to the faithful.
We will write and pray for all through the Cross.

September 6th 2014

The Lord called me -
Child – beloved daughter, carrier of the cross -
Be comforted by My Grace at work in you-
Be encouraged by My patient perseverance
To complete these icons for the glory of God.
Be blessed by My faith in the Father
To provide in all things.

Comment from 2022

Increasingly, as I surrendered to all that was being asked of me, I saw His mercy, Grace and Truth being lived out in me. To God alone be glory. Things that might have taken a lot of my time, were removed from my path ..... glory to God who knows all things. Every loss is gain.

I recall very little of the detail of this time, except the Grace I was being given to set up the small attic space to be an iconography studio, and to complete the icons that had been started on the courses with Aidan in Shropshire.

I do remember the conviction I was given to create the 'Key to the Door of Paradise' icon of the Theotokos, with a Golgotha in the background – not the Cross but the traditional rocks, and the cave with the skull. This was an indication of her awareness of Simeon's prophecy over Christ, and the prophecy that her heart too would be pierced. I started looking into the design of this but took the question with me when I went to the next icon course in September 2014 where Aidan Hart helped me.

Thursday 11th September 2014.

Walcott Hall Icon Course

Darkness
A birthing place-
Hope alive in Him who Lives.
No fear, but trust-
Patient perseverance,
And love for Him who saves.
Amen, Amen, Life and death united.

During the course, Aidan gave me a copy of an icon of his called 'Key to the Door of Paradise', which enabled me to understand the significance of the Golgotha background of my icon, bringing the foreground to represent 'Paradise'. Because of her purity, Mary, the Theotokos, was chosen to bear Christ, and thus is indeed 'The Key to the Door of Paradise'. Christ is the Door, but her purity was the Key to God's provision. Having been provided with these additional pieces I was able to proceed with the icon in my little studio.

Continual Prayer

Prayer. One of the prayer commitments that I had carried over from my Roman Catholic days, was the commitment of 9 days of prayer to a particular concern when prompted by the Holy Spirit.

So from 30th October – till 7th November, I was committed to praying for the Broken Hearted, both for particular people and more generally. As I had found before, I experienced more of my own broken-ness (or suffered with/for those I prayed for?). I found it was always turned to prayer for others who were feeling this despair, lostness and dread, and didn't know they could pray and ask for God's mercy and Spirit.

Maybe the event on November 24th was an answer to those prayers, as it was arranged that the priest and I would go to London to see the Archbishop.

November 24th 2014

The Priest and I travelled to London to see the Archbishop to ask him if he would make me a nun. At that meeting he said Yes, but I had responded 'wrongly' to the question, 'Are you committed to this parish?'. I had replied, 'God willing' when I meant, 'With God's help' – but I didn't know the correct 'form'!! The Archbishop made the priest my Spiritual Father.

The Archbishop wrote to the priest after the meeting, and my memory of the letter was: that we should wait a year, and if at the end of that time I wanted to leave, I would go with no blame; if I wanted to stay – then it would be done. The Priest remembered it as a NO…and maintained that without a monastery I could not be a nun.

I can see how God used this to make me more dependent on Him, rather than any position in the Church, but I felt the lack of the Spiritual blessing that comes through the Mystical Church and the Sacraments. And yet I see now (2023) that God was leaving a 'space' because He had more work in the depths to do!

And even giving me the Priest as my spiritual father, which I took seriously in terms of obedience, led me to deeper inner work and repentance, as I came to find the incongruence of our understanding of this role.

Comment from 2022

But here I was in the Parish – these are the facts! Let me provide some picture of the context I was serving and living in:

- Spiritually and with my free will, I surrendered to be obedient to the needs of the priest, and his plans and work for the parish and church;
- I was living in a multi-occupancy dwelling, 'Church House' initially with 5 men of various ages. We shared bathrooms and kitchens. My 'cell' and attic and back kitchen were part of the servants' wing of the Victorian Vicarage with a back staircase! I liked the hidden-ness of my small room overlooking the back garden.
- Both church and House were still on the journey of becoming what the priest and trustees wanted them to be. Many changes evolved during my 7 years here.
- The Church and Vicarage were opposite a park. The early morning walks with Beauty established me as part of a whole new circle of people…mainly of Asian origin – who were also out on their early morning walks to help their health. But I had to pray hard about the other later-in-the-day 'community' of the park that sometimes abused the provision and some of whom dealt in drugs.
- From very early on I was given a key to the church. (I was happy to recall the text, '*I would rather be the door keeper of the house of the Lord than dwell in the tents of the wicked*!!)
- I was starting to get to know people at the church, and formed a friendship with AA who was a Dr and also singer in the choir

> when she was free. This friendship developed over the 7 years I was there as we worked together on various projects and with particular families.

The Priest's request for a Resurrection 'icon' filling the end wall of the right-hand side aisle was part of the on-going development of the church. I was prompted to start drawing it in 2014 but it was not 'in action' till December 2015 and completed at Pentecost 2016. (It was always conceived in 'icon' terms because the wall on which it was to go was not one of the stone or brick walls of the church –it would therefore have been difficult to make it a 'fresco'....not least that I had no fresco experience to call on!)

From the beginning I started to visit a parishioner nearby, and heard something of her story, but then I was told via a 3rd person, I was 'too pious' and she didn't want me to visit. I simply kept praying...and some weeks afterwards texted her about something practical. Visiting was re-established and continues, 8 years further on.

Prayer life

I was invited by the priest to pray Matins and Vespers in the church and that continued for over 3 years. I began to get to know the Psalter better; and I was blessed to know more of the Saints.

I was trying again to learn the Greek alphabet and one day in **November 2014**, my eye caught an icon M...E...N...A...S. Menas. Two or three days later I saw it was the day of St Menas so I went to get the icon.

I needed to put the icon on a chair as the stand was elsewhere. Thus at the end of Matins I knelt down to honour the icon of St Menas. As I knelt there I was filled with Love coming to me via the icon, and I 'heard' in my heart, '*You were a martyr*'.

For the previous weeks I had been struggling with the anguish of the final abuse by my step-father, and both my head and heart had been without consolation, despite much prayer, repentance and forgiveness. But as these words reached my heart, it was embraced in Love, and then my mind received such consolation and release: truly all was redeemed. Glory to God.

The Mercy and Truth of God

And through St Menas' prayers
And Your merciful Love –
All changed by telling me
I was a martyr for Christ –
All shame gone through the Cross-
All mental anguish changed
To praise, love, thanksgiving
For allowing me to share
In the Love of God
For the world.

You are the God of my salvation
And I will worship you.

*We – One God – One Spirit- One Lord – One Hope-
One Joy- Oneness in Grace, Truth and Love,
Oneness in Joy, forbearance, forgiveness,
Jabez My beloved child, the Holy One of God.*

*Forgive your persecutors at all times and in
All places – if they hate Me, they will hate you –
Forgive and bless – be gentle and overcoming.
Pray at all times and love. Have faith child
That I will provide – MY heart overcoming/
Replacing yours. Amen daughter, Amen.*

Saturday 20th December '14

My cell at Church House, Kinston

Now in God's hands, I have Grace to surrender to life in this place – to prayer, book binding, iconography, and service in Love; my sense of Being – my boldness to proclaim Christ seems dead – and I live in faith, hope and (in faith) by His Love. I do not understand but I yield to this work. I have no sense of being except in prayer – but my doing is in prayer so I have to trust that even in the sense of Christ crucified I will live in Him in forgiveness and repentance and sorrow for sin.

Glory to God alone.

Christmas 2014

AA and I were blessed to put on a Christmas meal for singles or small families. We housed the meal in the Library in Church House and use its two kitchens for cooking. It was essentially bring and share and we had been given a donation of a large turkey and vegetables; and AA made a large salmon terrine for starters. We were not sure exactly how many there would be. In the end it was a total of 12, two families and one elderly man who had been told to come by one of the ladies who used to come to the Church's 'Thursday lunch club'. God bound us all together in love in wonderful ways. The elderly man had always longed to be a Father Christmas and he got to give out the small gifts that we had for everyone.

The whole feast started about 2 pm … I think the last coffee and mince pies were served about 9.30pm!! At one time I was falling asleep in the kitchen to the sound of AA discussing their faith with the two boys of the Greek family. We had 5 Nationalities there that Christmas!! It became an annual joy…but it was always different and always God gave us surprises and joy. He taught me to pray for harmony and love, despite the disparate people, languages and ages. And in Faith and absolute trust I focussed on the practicalities and He united all through the Holy Spirit.

Truly this was Grace in action. But He is a 'Wonderful Counsellor and Teacher' and He underlined the teaching when I went to the Monastery.

January 14th 2015

The Monastery

I was asked by the Spirit to consider

the Psychology of Grace:

In other words – what does the mind need to accept/think in order for GRACE to operate?

- God is bigger than my understanding
- God desires to work through me
- God carries the burden
- God delivers me from sin and selfishness
- God loves me and all things work together for good for the sake of those that love Him.
- God knows what needs to be done and will guide and instruct.

- **The Psychology of Sin** –(at least subconscious)
- I need to provide for myself
- Others will not provide
- There is no God who provides and loves
- My way is right because it covers my pain and loss
- I deserve pleasure.

My visit to the monastery had new dimensions since being in the Parish because there were questions being raised through my experiences. I believe this was the visit to the Monastery when I was being re-taught about the structure of the services! I had real need now to learn the elements that make up Matins and Vespers and the significance of them, as I now had access to more liturgical books.

Treasury of Blessings….

Each Word a gift of Love
Like a Divine Treasure Chest
Waiting to pour out its Secret Delights
Into open and hungry hearts,
Longing for the Healing touch
Of Divine Life in Grace
Through the Holy Spirit
In a surrendered mind.

Also while at the monastery I was asking questions about language – i.e. Greek, Romanian and Russian liturgical expressions. I was also asking about pastoral care of people I had been asked to 'care for'. And making candles – another task I had been asked to do!! Practical and Spiritual becoming unified in Love.

Extending my boundaries back at the Parish

The Parish Priest was asking me to share in the making of bi- and tri-lingual service books. I had to learn to get quite specific in what I needed him to supply to avoid drowning in my incompetence in technical things with which he could not help.

Overcoming in Love

I faced another brick wall of
'Not knowing' and I prayed!
And a glimmer of Light
Would show me a first step,
Or someone to ask...Step one-
Then revealed step two…
And then the careful,
Prayerful getting foreign words
Matching other foreign words –
With multiple 'accents' –
And English - in Love.
Always, for my own soul's sake
Seeking Action in and through
Love - seeking to bless in advance
Those who would use
The Memorial Service,
Or Funeral Service – in
Their own language.

'I wept when I was blessed to be present at a memorial service in Romanian and the woman, having lost her mother, was so moved and comforted to be able to pray in Romanian. Glory to God and the mercy of the Priest who wanted to provide for these mourning souls.' (Journal)

(**Comment:** We were working on the Funeral service in Greek and English for years, and finally produced multiple copies which have been used by many Orthodox churches around; it still awaits the blessing of the Archdiocese.)

But **Spring of 2015** meant facing the damage to my right shoulder, which the osteopath in France had warned me could be serious. I had largely been trying to ignore the pain since moving in.

I was given a scan at the Hospital in Kinston which revealed the torn shoulder cuff muscle, leading to an appointment with Mr S at the hospital on a Wednesday.

Learning to Ask. P (who helped in the office one day a week) and the Priest drove me down to the hospital. I was totally empty – and I think it was P who said that I should ask questions. I asked, 'what I should ask?' And one of the questions they suggested was 'What question should I ask you?' So with this 'in the world' support, and trusting in God to provide, I went in to the appointment.

Mr S affirmed my need for a 'cuff repair'…and maybe gave me more details – I know at one point he told me it was a serious operation done through key-hole surgery. At a silent point in our meeting, I asked, 'Is there a question I should be asking?' This is where God stepped in. Mr S began to tell me he had a long waiting list, then interrupted himself and said I could take the quick route if I was flexible, then interrupted himself again by picking up the phone and talking to his secretary.

He then told me to wait in the next room. After a while the secretary arrived and told me there was a cancellation for Monday, but she hadn't been able to book me in for the pre-op tests. But she would let me know if there were other cancellations and meanwhile, she would get the pre-op test arranged. I got on the bus to go back to town. Before getting to the bus station in Kinston, my phone rang, and I was told I needed to go back for 3pm for the pre-op tests, ready for a Monday operation!!!!

Not only did I get my tests done that afternoon, but I was able to witness to God's love, as I listened to the nurse pouring out her pain and disillusionment about her lost faith. God is indeed love.

The operation was on **2nd March** – and left me one handed!

By this time, I had offered **bookbinding classes** with the Priest's encouragement, and we were making some small case-bound copies of an English- Romanian Liturgy Book, as well as starting the sewing of sections for a Memorial Book that was wanted.

During the morning book-binding group of **April 8th** (in Holy Week), I finished the task of gluing cases and Liturgy books together. We were then called for lunch and went outside into the Spring sunshine. The Priest handed me a box of printer ink that had been delivered, so I ran to take it into the office.

The next thing I knew I had fallen over the second step into the porch– and heard a 'crack' in my left wrist as it hit the inside step into the house. Glory to God I did not hit or damage further my right shoulder.

Facing the Truth of Pain

Although the pain racked my body
And my wrist and hand spoke the damage;
Yet I had courage in my soul,
And total peace, even when told
'It's not damaged – it's OK…'

But mercy took me to the hospital,
And nurse-practitioner confirmed
The Collis fracture…and the need
To pull it straight – then plaster!
I was being allowed to suffer
Something of Christ's Suffering.

Indeed 'all will be well'...as day
By day I yielded to His Grace to
Overcome the pain and difficulties –
Of getting up, getting dressed,
And providing for my basic needs.

In God's mercy a young woman
From Romania took over hair care,
And plaited it and fastened it up.
With a hat in place, it lasted
a long time! Humility and Patience
In total mystery and surrender.

I didn't intend pridefulness – but because I did not realise the significance of resting my broken arm, (when resting anything that moved was difficult!) when I went back after the week, I had to have it re-splintered because it was still swollen. They gave me a more inviting sling which was more comfortable to wear, and strict instructions to keep it up and rested to allow the swelling to go down!! I still don't know how I got through this time, except by Grace. The Holy Spirit taught me many ways of getting clothes on within the limits of one damaged shoulder and the other broken wrist!!

The repercussions of this break and shoulder operation lasted a long time as I then had a complication with a 1 in 200 'gift' of a fractured thumb tendon accompanying the Collis fracture. The Kinston hospital referred me straightaway to the Hand-Clinic of the hospital in the city when my plaster came off and they saw my helpless thumb! I attended that Hand Clinic for months – first getting the wrist and arm and hand working again and flexible enough to be able to be plastered up again after the replacement thumb tendon operation .....etc etc...

Also in **April** 2015 Beauty was bitten in the park when someone else had taken her out and she needed vet treatment – (thanks to the kindness of a resident) in getting us there). Although the wound healed quite quickly, the wound of her soul was visible for a long time. She changed from her very friendly, trusting self to being wary of aggressive actions!

I also found myself buying half a **grave, making my will** and buying a Funeral Plan in February 2015. I never questioned this but accepted that it would mean I was taking responsibility for my death and would not be a burden to anyone!!

Some of the inner turmoil I was becoming aware of was the sense of 'being in the way' or 'not being wanted' stemming from childhood. I prayed a lot to ensure I was not projecting past history – but seeking to be pure of heart in seeking to see things through God's eyes. So whenever I discerned these feelings – I invited Christ into the darkness, so my lack of love or trust in God could be repented of, and then I could pray in Love for the whole situation.

I was aware of my desire to pursue a life of prayer.

Partly because of our Iconography, and Scottish connection, a Nun I knew was in my thoughts, as she became Orthodox and was seeking to become an Orthodox nun. Around **September 2015,** I was invited to rent a small, terraced house along the road from the church with a view to it becoming a house of prayer with this nun. She came with me to the Monastery in the Autumn, and we discussed this with the Igumeni (the Abbess).

I moved into this delightful terrace house with an enclosed back garden with trees, and a pond. I had a free hand to make good the electrics, and over the first four months, got a partition put into the large back bedroom, making it a 3-bedroom house. I used the back cell, gained through the corridor that now also gave access to the 2nd bedroom.

I had high hopes for this Prayer House, which then fell, when this nun was advised to go to a monastery on a Greek island. Here she would receive formation as a Greek Orthodox nun, and develop her iconography. Meanwhile, I had taken, in good faith, and at a City Priest's request, a 'lodger'. It became clear after some months that we were not spiritually in tune, and I was not in a position to help her. (I now realise she was probably severely traumatised and needed more than I could give.) At the end of a year – I came back to a large room in Church House and a Romanian family were able to take the house for a year.

I had still been doing all the work that the Priest was asking while in the little house and was preparing the design for the Resurrection wall as agreed with the Igumeni of the Monastery.

So, in **December of 2015 the boards for the wall size 'icon' of the Iconostasis** (Resurrection) were prepared by the joiner, M, – then taken down and placed in the room in the church, where iconography had been moved to.

There is only commitment and love associated with the prayer and joy of the careful preparation of the marine-ply boards in 5 sections. Iconography is almost as much about preparation and prayer as the ultimate product or image. It's a Grace of prayer, labour and Love, Truth and Mystery beyond knowing. I have just found photos of this time, J* pouring herself into careful filling of unwanted holes in the marine ply – and D and her gessoing the boards one layer at a time

(*J was a long-standing member of the congregation, then in her 80s, who had worked in the leather factory in Kinston as a young woman and married a Serbian man who was Orthodox. Although she never extended her Anglican roots to 'Orthodoxy', she had been attending the Orthodox services with her husband for years, and after his death, in Kinston. She had a strong connection to the Divine and would frequently tell me who I needed to talk to, or what I should give someone at the end of a Sunday service. I learned to be obedient to her requests (really commands!) and in Love they were always a blessing to those she identified as being in need.)

But back to her work with the big icon...Gradually it was made ready for painting: with gessoing finished, and sanding done by J, D and myself...

The process of getting the images 'blown up' by a printer came via help from Shrewsbury iconographers, and the images were finally transferred onto the boards. …

I worked every day after Matins and started with the two side pieces depicting hell. I lived that desolation of the soul. The design on these, following the suggestion of the Priest, was based on World War 1 photographs – given that the Memorial Boards in the centre of the 'icon' commemorated local soldiers, who died during the 1st World War. The four images depicted different facets of the soul 'in hell'.

I had help with painting one or two days a week, and both D and the young Romanian, Ma, would arrive and ask for the prayer that prepared all iconography work. Only towards the end of the process did Ma tell me of the difference the prayer made to his shaking smoker's hand. D grew almost visibly in discernment and grace as he took on initially the task of all the borders, and Ma the detailed work of the New Jerusalem. But the prayer bound us all together in respect and love and they grew in true confidence and grace. (J had decided she would not be involved in the painting, though she had been asked.)

I 'knew' this Icon was to be ready for the Saturday of Souls before Pentecost so for about the last month, I did an Akathist (I think at 6.30am) then painted for 2 hours – did Matins and continued.

I tried to make a list of what was needed one morning!! I was rebuked, very gently, by the Holy Spirit – and I surrendered, so I was simply led… and 'all manner of things became well'. I was not surprised when the icon was ready to be hung in time for final touching up ready for the Saturday of Souls. But I was inordinately grateful.

June 11th 2016

Resurrection

You and I, we…carefully formed,
Being made into His likeness
With all sorts of loving interventions,
That challenged an over-growth,
Or shortfall, so it could be re-thought
And given new life.

And eventually on the Saturday of Souls
The completed boards were put into place
With large scaffolding at different
Heights for M to do his work.

All I could offer were prayers for those
Carrying the sections and -
Lifting them to M. Only God knows
How many angels were with us –
But the task was done.
The Resurrection surmounting and
Surrounding the Memorial boards
Of the 1st World War bringing hope and love.
And anointed by the Archbishop when he next came.
And he called me an Iconographer.
Glory to God.

Comment from 2022

Although this 'work' had an effect on the outside, it had built me in faith, trust and grace on the inside. And I suspect I had felt something of the fullness of the work of the Holy Spirit, through prayer, through Godly purpose, through unity working with others, and through the Lord developing my grace and technical skill as an iconographer. I falsely assumed that this would grow further.

5

Staying Still and Accepting Disappointment: Obedience to Death

Acceptance of Disappointment

I had applied for and
Hoped to join the 3 year course
Of Iconography, rooting and grounding
Me in this form of God's love and service.
And I was accepted.
But when I sought support, I was told No..
But I could have Church supported tutorials
For specific Icons with Aidan.
I accepted without a fuss.
But the child within sensed the loss
Of like-minded travellers – once more
Needing to accept the lonely road.

7th September 2016

Meeting with Aidan:
I was 'at ease' when I saw Aidan,
He knows monastic life and thinking,
And I am purely loved by him.
He judged me not, but would guide me
In iconography according to how much
I could receive!!
And he heard the story, and accepted
My obedience…but was sorry.
He gave me courage to continue
Moving forward with the unknown elements of
St Marina, and the design for St Joseph.
He guided me once more to look to
The hands and eyes!!*

*Aidan had great Grace to forebear with the slowness of my development. Only as more of my soul and ability to 'see' surrendered to the Cross was the Holy Spirit able to give me Grace, Patience and the humility of careful attention, rather than 'knowing' for the many crucial elements of both figure and other icon elements. Lord have mercy.

So I accepted the discipline of work on icons and on the computer. These now included 3-monthly Service Sheets; Baptism booklets in Romanian or English to give out after Baptism services (ensuring families were provided with an understanding of Christ's love and provision in bringing the child into 'the Church'); and continuing work on the bi- and tri-lingual services.

Internal Trials bring External Courage Through Prayer

The Lord responded to me in Aug 2016 when I was asking for courage and strength:

> *'Despised and rejected – a man of grief and acquainted with sorrows'*
> *Child- the depth of your sorrows humanly is great –*
> *And is the cause of your half-heartedness and weakness.*
> *Many share this pain, and your prayers and love*
> *In Me brings hope and healing to many.*
> *Do not deny your pain – rejoice that it is the source of love and healing for others.*
> Oh Lord! Thank you for my losses that through Your Precious Cross they are the source of prayer, understanding, mercy and love for broken hearts.
>
> (It's true…my understanding and compassion for the Romanian families came through the Grace and Love He was giving me.)

Learning Greek: Another aspect of my learning since being here was learning Greek because of the number of parishioners who spoke Greek. I had spent 5 weeks in 2016 with AS, who I had initially got to know while in Edinburgh with Father John Maitland Moir. This first visit started in Thessaloniki but finished with four weeks in the village. I spent 3 of these days at Ormylia Monastery, where Fr John Maitland Moir used to visit, and had been well-loved. My current Priest had given me a blessing to try and find out if any monasteries would accept me. I visited many amazing sites including Meteora monasteries with AS and her son. Many more blessings, including very old frescoes, iconography and building wonders, but no open doors.

During a three day stay at Ormylia I was blessed with an un-asked for 'interview' with the priest! He gave me various suggestions for monasteries, and people to ask, all of which I fulfilled in the following weeks, but the answer was always NO …and usually, 'you are too old!!'

Love your Neighbour

God also brought into my life dear and soul-refreshing friends. One retired Anglican priest who I met through Aidan's icon courses, asked me to help him finish the many unfinished icons he had started during the week-long courses with Aidan. We met regularly for iconography sessions either at his house, or he came to Church House. He did finish a number of icons, and I was blessed with encouragement of the Grace I was given, and a 'child of God' friend.

Also Penny, who was brought to me by the Priest - with her I shared impromptu evenings and prayer; and gatherings with Maria whom God brought to the church when she was convicted by God of not going to church. She was a Greek nurse working at the Kinston Hospital for a period, and first came to one of the Vespers services. And another Greek Maria who was in Kinston for her academic work. We shared time together too.

I was also gradually getting to know the families of the Church. It was interesting to see how the very fact of 'families' etc would bring to the Light unhealed bitterness, or unwillingness to serve 'when I had never received' the love they had! Of course, in prayer the Lord showed me and touched me with His love. But He was teaching me – giving me more of His Love….to grow in Love and Grace.

'I was having to learn to temper my expectations of people! I thought that everyone in the church wanted to live for Christ in increasing purity and grow in the fruit and gifts of the Spirit. But of course, I had a plank in my own eye too – when I did not seek to understand their lives, difficulties, church, and spiritual experience and love them in Christ…' (Journal)

As more Romanian couples came to bring babies for baptism, the

Priest and his fellow -priest needed to develop formal baptism applications with forms, responding to the needs of the Arch-Diocese Baptismal Certificates; and eventually needing to charge to ensure Archdiocese and church costs were covered.

My role in baptisms changed over the years. However, in the last few years, I did what I could to enable the 2nd priest to keep going by helping families prepare for the baptism, getting the water filled, and emptied, and filling in the forms. Some Saturdays (after the Covid lockdown opened up) there would be 10 or 11 baptisms for him to do. This was when the Priest was out of action because of one of his operations.

I learned greater and greater patience with those who wanted the service 'like we Romanians do it' when what they really meant was 'like we do it in our family at home'. But in being willing to love them where they were, I was given greater love and patience. I was able to bless, instead of being self-righteous and leaving them unhappy… Lord have mercy. But to God be the glory!!

But let me go back: In 2017, I had been asked at short notice to paint an icon of an Irish saint, St Palladius, so the Priest could give it as a gift during the Pilgrimage to Northern Ireland he was planning.

I remember I was unsure about whether to go on this pilgrimage or not. I got on with the icon of St Palladius and producing the Morning and Evening prayer booklets required. The poetry here reflects some awareness of difficulty and yet being held by God.

July 1st 2017

Irish Pilgrimage
Metaphorically
Walking on water –
I travelled to Dublin –
Floating in a mass of happening-
Not knowing where I was-
But present in Rostreva –
On a pilgrimage to
Ireland and parts of Eire-
As we looked for footsteps
Of St Bridget, and St Patrick.
My soul rejoiced in their
Nearness and our Oneness
With them in Christ.
Yet in my soul
Was pain and loss
And hidden hurt.

July 3rd

The pain gnaws at my heart
Ending my deadness
And making way for prayer
And transforming Grace.

The yearning for love,
Intimacy, a human heart
With which to share the seeking,
Knocking, asking - over whelms me.

Yet I am given grace
To face, acknowledge, accept
This emptiness and loss of face-
To accept with Grace, this death.

In Love Divine I pray
For the broken and lost.
The dumb and broken-hearted,
The blind who do not know the Way.

Comment from 2022

Meanwhile hospital visits continued, and October 2017 brought the second thumb operation (injection). On the inside I was facing deeper and deeper awareness of the pain and degradation of my childhood. By His Grace, I was faithful to His Love for me, and regardless of how I was feeling, I knew that NOW I could bring all that to the Cross, to praise and receive His love and healing. And with all my heart I refused to project the pain onto others – but it was only possible through owning the pain, and prayer.

Owning the Pain

I felt a piercing of my heart-
Dividing me from love, compassion
And understanding, and
I began to pray.

Lord You have told me You will not rest
Till Your salvation shines out from me
Like a Light: Come Holy Spirit, bring
Your Light into this darkened heart
And set me free from all self-interest.

Father forgive them
They knew not what they did,
And let me rejoice in this trial
According to Your Word-

And let my heart explode
With the fire of Your Love
Burning up all the thorns
Of my intransigence.

Lord have mercy on us,
Lord Jesus Christ have mercy.
Let Your Love prepare me for rest,
And trust in Your Love in me
For the morning. Amen

Comment from 2022

I would pray the Jesus prayer until **my** heart was at peace, and I knew I would be open in Love, to whatever the following day would bring. Glory to God for His mercy and provision.

A second visit to Greece in **Summer 2017** was for 2 weeks at AS's village house in a village in Halkidiki, north of Thessaloniki.

The broken car, became a blessing
As day by day, we gently walked
To the church, or to the village –
And AS chatted with 'old lady'
Friends of such courage,
Graciousness, and surrender.
'Den pirasi.' …'It doesn't matter'
'Malista'…..Certainly – Ok
These words punctuating
The unknown, with Grace.
Or we got a bus, and valued
The simple coffee in a square
While waiting for the next bus.
Life unfolding at a slow pace.

Then in **November of 2017** I was encouraged and blessed to go for a further 5 weeks to Thessaloniki, for more formal lessons of Greek. I lodged with AS who had arranged lessons for me. Poverty was everywhere and there were many beggars around the local church which had both a food bank, and clothes to provide for the needy. I had the joy of meeting more of her friends and joining in prayer.

And I loved the joy and freedom of having lessons everyday – and surrendering to God's Grace surrounded by the Beauty of Love and Life!

28th December 2017

AA and I had another shared Christmas
With those without wider family -
Though little time to organise it, - but
With all the Love and blessings
Embedded in surrender
To God's Grace, love and mercy,
All manner of things were well.

1st January 2018

(I had been prompted to buy an A5 size Moleskin Diary for 2018 and I had wondered WHY? Then I had a sense I was to give time to listen to the Holy Spirit and write in the relatively small space for each day.)

> *We, us, One in Jesus Christ, hidden in God the Father – by the Holy Spirit.*
> *Seek, knock, ask and pray at all times, for MY Face, Light, Truth and Love. Peace be with you. Amen*

Each day was Divine instruction, encouragement, or loving rebuke with direction, always building and enabling the Holy Spirit to guide. Truly these were nuggets of 'Gold'. During the day, I would often be in a situation that needed the teaching of that day.
I was constantly made aware of how this Divine teaching was truly 'Alive' in the Spirit, and made firstly a difference to my Spirit in keeping me calm, loving, or wise, and, secondly, preventing 'sin and division' with others because I had no animosity.

Alongside these encouragements to me to TRUST in God's Grace alive in me, there was continuation of work for the church, and other medical appointments!!

Some appointments stemmed from an investigation of my difficulties 'swallowing'; and the osteoporosis of my spine; and foot/ankle problems!!

I was following up my Greek lessons, and had joined the class at a church in the city.

February 2018

A meeting with the Priest which was 'work' focussed. This seems to be the first mention of the 12 great Feasts, the Festal Icons of the Church.

For Lent I committed myself to a list of items needing work - including renewal of the Vespers and Matins booklets used in the Church, and doing work in the garden on the raspberry canes!!

Shifting Ground

Change was in the air, but I lived for Christ crucified and I accepted all things that did or did not happen, until God revealed the Way. For the most part I lived with this as 'awareness' but without judgement or bitterness.

Serving the Broken Hearted

One element of the Way was the relationship I had developed with the **Wheelhouse Community in Nottingham.** They were a group of women who had got together to support each other through prayer in relation to their (largely adult) children who had mental health problems, or their own mental health problems. Fr Stephen (an old Spiritual father, blessed by Fr John Maitland Moir to be a support) had invited me to join him over in Nottingham with them one Sunday for lunch.

I had arrived in time for lunch, enjoyed meeting and listening to people of the group and finally spent time with SW, a key figure. By 6pm everyone else had gone and after time with SW, I had accepted God's invitation to offer support through prayer and visits. I made initial visits to discover the activities they offered for those they supported. The Priest of Kinston blessed me to spend 3 or 4 days at a time with them every 6 weeks or so.

Bringing the Unseen Real!

We met for prayer,
Or creating cards to bless others,
And I listened to people
Who needed an ear of Love.

I would feel totally empty
When I went but the Lord
Would enable them to feel Peace,
Courage or with some…JOY!!!

He provided for their needs
Out of my emptiness!!

Moving out for Major Change.. Over the previous 4 years I had needed to move the Iconography space, at least every year. Now it was being made clear that we needed to move out of Church House totally by **September 2018** so they could start the refurbishment of the house.
My iconography materials were already back in my church house room. My room was a mess – not least because I was still seeking to offer God ALL my time, including time that might have been used for re-organising!!

I had booked two **flights to Athens in relation to Maria's wedding.** Maria, now back in Athens, was getting married and wanted her guests to be blessed with an appropriate Word of God. On the first flight I was taking the 'Word of Life' hand-sewn sachets to contain an icon of Christ and Words from Holy Scripture and John Chrysostom. I needed to deliver them before the wedding so we could complete putting them together. I was also trying to tidy my room and finish an icon!

My first flight was booked for the afternoon of **Wednesday 27th, June** 2018 and that morning, early, I got an email to say it was cancelled. I was shocked, but prayed and did what I needed, which involved a long phone call to re-book a flight. In God's grace I got a flight for the following morning from the city airport, at 07.55.am. As I breathed a sigh of relief, and 'thank You', I felt called to kneel and pray.

> As I listened, I hear God say,
> ***'I want you to commit yourself to***
> ***this church in obedience to Me.'***
>
> At that moment the Priest
> Knocked the door to give me a card
> To take to Maria.
> I told him what God had said to me,
> Even as tears were still falling.
>
> Deep in my being, I sensed I had been
> Asked to turn a corner.
> GOD asked me to re-commit to loving
> The people of the Church,
> And be 'obedient to Him'.

So, I took the card for Maria, packed my case, gave some of the extra time to the icon I wanted to finish, and tidied up some of the mess. Glory to God.
And the following morning I caught my flight knowing that I had already booked a mini- trip to the Greek island monastery on 5th-6th July as part of my time in Athens so -

Going with God

I went with lightness of heart
And total trust that God
Would show the way.
And was blessed on the way to Athens
With two days with dear friends from Scotland
Who now lived permanently
Back home in Vienna.
And then my mini two days visit
To the Monastery on the island.

The talk with the Igumeni of this Monastery was very clarifying. Firstly in 'confessing' to her all the stress, and the pain of seeking to purify my thoughts and intentions, over the last few years, I received great Peace....a sense of 'It is finished'.

But she also made it plain that although I was welcome to come for hospitality, they were not taking in any more non-Greek novices for now. So although I could have gone out to the monastery when I had to leave Church House I did not feel in my Spirit that this was God's will.

After spending some time with my nun friend, now a novice of the monastery, I spent the night down at the tiny monastery just below the Parent Monastery. Although I spent uncomfortable early hours having eaten something that disagreed with me, I really sensed the grace of God with me. When daylight came, I was not afraid of my weakness, or the recurring attacks and walked a little outside despite feeling very weak...

Finally, the Russian Novice nun appeared to do what she needed outside, and I was able to ask for help. Between various translation Apps on our phones, we managed to communicate. She warned the Main monastery of my state, and I was told they had something for me to take and would provide when they came to pick me up.

Walking round the courtyard in Grace and faith in the morning sun, strengthened me beyond the unutterable weakness I had felt, and by the time I was driven back to the main Monastery…I was ready for the tablet they gave me and a rice lunch, away from everyone else.

I felt the love from everyone and received such kindness – expecting to have to get the bus from the town to the airport but no- they drove me all the way there.
And when I was there, I checked my messages and emails. I had received a message from Aidan Hart telling me of St Julian's Tower in Shrewsbury and that I may be able to stay in in September. God provides.

And in Athens, staying with Maria, I was blessed with a visit to two churches near the ancient centre, whose priests had known my Spiritual Father from Edinburgh. So I was blessed beyond words, through Heavenly Truths of unity…. and the kindness of Maria and Stephan in sharing ice-creams, and then lunch out in the shaded sunshine. I returned to Kinston refreshed for a move.

I made arrangements to visit the owner of St Julian's Tower, and despite my misgivings, I was given strength to climb the steps of the tower up to the various levels. My knees did not complain!! I was blessed to accept the levels – and to see how I could make them viable….and to use the old church for prayer. I immediately wanted to make an icon of St Juliana, (my original baptismal name was Gillian) and for St Alkmund, in whose church, in Derby, I had originally been baptised as a child. His church was next door to St Juliana's. I sensed God bringing restoration in deeper parts of my being.

Time to Move?

More packing and planning:
More boxes labelled for St Julian's
And Icons for the Church space:
And plans to get rid of furniture?
What to do?
And meanwhile keeping praying
And trusting the Holy Spirit
To uphold and bless not just me
But all the souls in the house
Who had to surrender to the unknown
And give up the comfort of the love
That had bound us.

12th – 17th September 2018

Athens

I went to Athens for Maria's wedding – Glory to God for all those I met and came to love.

17th to 20th September

Vienna

I returned via Vienna to supplement the shortened stay during the previous visit.

It was a blessing to spend more time with Christina and Frederic, the latter getting more feeble but still able and willing to walk. I determined to be open to what they offered for love of God the Father, and Christina and Frederic took me round bits of Vienna by public transport. It was a joy to see the Churches and enjoy an oversized ice-cream… and the amazing cake and coffee shops of Vienna. We only went in to one of them – but discovered their gluten free options!!! We also walked in parks and watched enormous goldfish in a park pond! I was so glad I was given Grace to enjoy what they and Vienna were blessed to offer. God is Good.

Back to KINSTON.

I got back by Thursday evening and spent Friday and Saturday getting all things ready to move things to St Julian's Tower, or to store.

Sunday 23rd September 2018

After liturgy, the Priest asked me to go to see them at their house. They told me I could have the 'housekeepers flat' and stay put without having to move.

God worked miracles – and kept me 'still' in the place He had provided. God is good. Glory to God.

6

Staying Still, in Order to Love in Christ : In Obedience to God the Father

Reflection on Change!

Having lived in community for 5 years, with shared spaces, awareness for each other and all the swings and roundabouts of 4 or 5 different nationalities and languages in daily communion with each other -something of life seemed to stop when all moved out! But certainly change did not stop, along with the need to respond!

9th October 2018

In God alone I put my trust*.
Come Lord Jesus –
Come Holy Spirit-
If You desire me to write
-to witness to You
To provide for others
To leave a legacy –
Then Lord I ask You to
Fill me and lead me.

Lead me through
All the potentially conflicting
Things – that I may
Fulfil Your desire and need
For my life in You.

Child – you have prepared a Way –
It is enough for today –
Get dressed – go and work on your icon-
Give Me all those you pray for, and be blessed
In My Silence and Love.

*I had heard and sensed some months back that I would not move from the house – but I had presumed nothing…till I was told that I did not have to move.

Summary of the Context of October 2018 to end of 2019

Making a Way of Integrity

Imagine dear Reader a large-multi-occupancy house
And think of its innards providing life!!
Heating , lighting and plumbing added to, changed,
And modified over the years since the 1900s!!

The vertical slice cut through the right-hand side
Of the building was to be my dwelling
It included the 3-storey servants quarters ,
With added first floor front bedroom.

Sounds easy…but that meant plumbing and wiring
Being made intrinsic to this Flat 7.
I would shut myself away at 'work'
While investigation and internal excavation
Went on…and by God's Grace clear
The dust and mess each evening.

Comment 2023

Dear Reader – we could take this as a metaphor for our body and soul too! All those experiences, and ways of thinking we have learned that are attached to other people or false gods!! And God wants to restore our soul to 'integrity' and obedient to Him. Come Lord Jesus – be our vision and hope as we continue our YES to God the Father.

Monday 7th January 2019

Suffering in the depths every morning
Till prayer, praise and the Holy Spirit
Lift me to Life Eternal.
Yet today called back to the Listening Place
To go into the depths to face 'the crown of thorns' -

(St Menas kissed my forehead
and spoke 'Crown of Thorns' –
Through this maybe I come to understand
more of 'the Glory of God'?)

Crown of Thorns

No name to call my own –
No home of my own on earth –
No immediate friends or family to stand with me-
Aware of all I can/could give
Yet not blessed, to do so.
Loving and obedient to God the Father
So 'No' is not an option and I choose
To make this crucifixion my will.

I am alone without close soul friend to walk this path with me.
I feel despised and rejected – even in Love.
I had hopes – dreams – all my human grace is given.

The Lord speaks Isaiah 9:6 into my heart which is the verse after the prophecy concerning the birth of Christ. So 9:6 foretells of His government and peace – and that 'the zeal of the Lord of hosts will perform this'.

Then the Lord spoke:

Mary – My child from birth – despised and rejected by men – but taken up by God – My daughter from before birth; formed and taught by My Spirit, transformed from death to life, many times.- purified – a living Magnificat.

You will bring them to Me (the Women of the Wheelhouse) in righteousness and grace. I see and hear their wants, but I want to provide for their needs. But today, let Me provide for your needs. – in the sanctuary. Do not let your heart be troubled.
What stops you writing?

Other tasks for the church

Icons (*Part of writing)*

I don't want to be contentious or to cause conflict (*Speaking the Truth in Love leads to Harmony for those who seek it)*

There is so much to write and I don't know where to start..*(Let Me work)*

I am afraid – what shall I do with it? Who is it for? *(This is hidden in Christ, in God; Obedience is the first step.)*

Growing up to stand for what you need:

1. At least one day a week cloistered to write;
2. 2 half days for icons
3. Daily Prayer, Matins and Vesper and midday Jesus prayer.- and continual prayer.
4. 2 half days for Parish visiting-
5. Set availability for calls – like a monastery.

Comment on the Above from July 2022

Only later I realised I had not presented my needs to the Priest – and I just grabbed time as it appeared vacant, though it was easier to assert time for icons because it overtly served the parish. I did start deliberately making time for Parish visits.

Persevering in Faith and trust

The changes going on all around were part of life, but not easy to live with.

The office was still in the house for some months into 2019 creating security problems – and problems with those who did not understand boundaries.

One young man the priest was trying to help with work in **March 2019,** took advantage of the open doors during the day and came into the kitchen. I was shocked and made it clear this was private. But when I was at church doing Vespers, he came and stole my bag and computer from my room upstairs, probably getting in through the back door which I had not checked before I went out. The material loss was not what left a mark, but the sense of insecurity, and not being protected, underlined an existing wound…thus bringing more dark to the Light.

One evening after this happened, I was in the kitchen and saw the face of this man in the back garden peering at me… and the fear went through me like a knife! I checked all doors etc – which were locked...but it wasn't an easy time.

Finding Humour and Love!!

The trenches outside had to be seen to be believed, at the front across the lawn, and in front of the house for sewage, gas, water and electric, and at the back, rerouting sewage and water pipes! I came to love B and his workman - all Georgians…. One evening I returned to my back entrance and had to cross a trench to get to my back door. C had put a bridge for me (an old door I think) – with a pot of flowers on it to make me think of Venice!!

So despite the inconvenience, there was humour and kindness. I used to buy dark chocolate for the young men who were digging, for hours sometimes, because care had to be taken in digging the trenches in order to find an existing pipe or cable. And on a Friday I would sometimes join Borea and team for a glass of wine at the end of the week.

Trials added up and brought their own fruit!!

The entries in July.. Dear READER – wrap yourself in the Love of God if you have suffered abuse trauma. But remember as you pray, God is with you….

Tuesday 2nd July

'– trials of more moving of stuff– physical weakness – and spiritual attack…' (But I finished praising….)

Sunday 21st July

Sitting with God.. The ramparts broken down – only the Cross, only defeat of all my gifts – only lovelessness on one hand and unutterable Love and Patience and Compassion on the other.... Glory to God.

Thursday 25th July 2019

I accept the Cross:
Joyful anticipation -
I am not alone.

Friday 26th July 2019

(Shown the agony of the broken heart today- trying to find a way to God.)

The curse of Adam,
Blaming Eve -Now Love cried out-
Sinless may stone her.

Sunday 28th July

(This included simple accounts of the sins against me by my step-father – up to the point before I lost consciousness the last time.) "You moved him away. He left me for dead. Who cleared me up? Who revived me? I know the Theotokos came to me – and has taught me in Your Name Lord."

The Wounds left alive
I am not allowed to complain-
I cannot fight for my own life-
I must withdraw from all life-giving activity because others will crush me;
I will always put love first;
I cannot deny my own cross- and the dereliction of my soul;
I don't know how to live for You.

Dear Reader: Do you see what gift this is?
I would never have seen these subconscious wounds without the gift of the 'trials' and desire to keep faithful to God. Some of them have Truth within them.... But in terms of turning to God...we **must** bring these things to God and seek His response.

Tuesday 6th August

Waves push, or pull me;
Undercurrent drags me down;
Above a star lifts.

Transfiguration Day – Come Holy Spirit

I was using the large front room for iconography, and the small 'housekeepers cupboard' for book binding and messy gluing etc of small paper icons. Until:

August 14th 2019

The drills are still hammering the walls in the main house – but today given a message. I need to clear the large front room so the men can get in next week to re-wire. This means packing up my iconography materials and making access to the floor. Glory to God for His Grace.

Gentling body – soul,
Uniting all, the Spirit
Lifts up to Heaven.

Thursday 26th September 2019

I was reminded I had promised St Seraphim to write poetry to lift and purify my mind – Forgive me Lord I do not do it enough.

> Waiting, wanting root,
> But I have received my need,
> My Lord embraces me.

Update on flat after a few weeks... The bulk of the filth, dust and restoring labour of the flat is complete as I know it – but unofficially told all this is temporary – but in Christ I have no fear.

Thus as the process worked on, the front door of Flat 7 was cut through a lower area near the kitchen onto the side passage up the Right of the house. Other changes also signalled.... I left all possibilities in God's hands. Today is enough!!

In November I travelled to Oxford to a day conference on St Maria Skobtsova. She had become a solitary nun in Paris and I had been reading her 'Spiritual Writings' which re-enforced elements of 'growing' in limited human love through calling on the Holy Spirit's Infinite Resource.

In 2019 the new Archbishop was appointed and in November I wrote to ask if I could see him.

On **December 10th 2019 I went to see the Archbishop** to ask him about becoming a nun.

His answer was clear - the Greeks don't make solitary nuns, though he recognised the Russians do! In response to questions, I had told him what I did in the Parish, and what role I was playing in Nottingham. He asked me if I was happy in the parish work. He then suggested I start a ministry for women in Kinston, and told me about the work of Mother Nectaria in Kolcata.

But I knew not the way...

Letter to God

Dear God, the Father,

…You do not leave me-
My life is tied to Yours my Lord
And You feed me by Your Word
Enlightening Your crucifixion to me;
I forgive, forgive and forgive.
I forbear, and bless and
Ask you to extend my boundaries like Jabez.
Where my God can I go -
You have the Words of Eternal Life...?
I wait for power from on High.
So until You Bless me,
I focus on the icon of the Annunciation
and I hope in Your Grace for You to Carry me,
Lead me, and give me grace to keep forebearing, blessing
And above all forgiving.
I understand nothing but Christ crucified.

I blame no-one – I made the decision to become Orthodox –
I agreed with every step –
No man can help me. No man can be my father in this world-
Only God, Father, Son and Holy Spirit can complete their work-
In and through me. Your will be done my God.
So I thank you Father for the trials of the last five and a half years.
Thank You for breaking open prison cells and bringing into the Light-
The 'hell' of my conception, threat on my life, and childhood.
To You alone be glory.

Papa, I know You are answering a prayer that I prayed –
To be able to be received in Love when I die –
And that I would suffer what I needed to suffer in this life
In order to be acceptable to Your Eternal Kingdom ----
I just wish it wasn't so painful!!

Now I want you to do a new work child. I want your silence to expand with your love. I want you to grow into a giant of Grace – morning, noon and night, allowing Me a free hand to use you 'full of Grace' for My purposes – without shame or fear. I will provide for your needs.

In front of all evil, including self-pity, silently praise and pray and offer no rational or Spiritual wisdom. Those with ears to hear will hear the silent wisdom, and otherwise will receive My gentle love in their pain.
This is all child. Go and get on with the icon presentation. I love you.

At Christmas 2019

The Christmas meal was held in the Church Hall and food brought over from the back kitchen. We had about 12 people, two families, some singles and 6 nationalities and from photographs – many cracker-hats!!!! Glory to God.

2020

The Garden – By the grace of God I was moved in January to go and ask for some garden space because all the gardens are being sectioned off and access to the back garden cut off because of changes. I was led to go with a sense of 'being a child of God, who could ask for such things'…I was given the ground which would become the garden of Flat 8, the flat I had hoped for myself.

It became a life saver as it gave me an active outlet of the Grace God gave me to make something beautiful, good, and true. The area given had been a number of rubbish heaps and included abandoned bathtub, tiles and bricks! But it also included a peach tree and an olive tree (given many years ago by Paraskevi). In some senses it fed my soul as I was enabled to plan, re-create, and make good this waste area of the whole garden. Apart from this I had no control except over my responses to things, but this gave me something renewing…as a Child of God... 'Effectiveness' and fresh air and re-connecting with the birds and animals were very restorative. When I needed help to set the appropriate boundaries of this garden, (and provide shade for the 'pond' – made from the bath-) B and his men helped me make a fence out of pallets (and I paid for their time). By the time it was painted with wood preservatives the pallets became united!! But I get ahead of myself.

Women's Ministry

Covid was looming large on the horizon even by January 2020, but before the shutdown happened, I had enrolled the help of ML a young women from the Parish who had relevant experience and knowledge of women who suffered. She taught me about the systems in place and hostels for women in need in Kinston area. There was no ministry through the local churches, only the Council-run Women's Safe Refuge House for those who needed escape from abusive partners.

As ML and I were discussing our options and what the women needed, all doors of face to face interaction shut in March because of Covid infections.

I had already been doing women's work with some individuals and the wives of couples with families in the parish context. Many women I got to know in the parish had an abusive past or present, though often 'kept behind closed doors'. I have to give God the glory for these meetings. He just led me to people – at a point when they had need!! It was as if in my emptiness, He provided His love and Strength!!

The following poem reflects the truth of God's love for one woman He led me to…But He always pointed those I went to, to Christ's Way to deal with things: I thought I was just taking Paracetamol!.

The Unexpected Baby Sitter

Nothing is impossible for God;
And here I was with little experience
Of playing with little children;
But this visitor with paracetamol
Became a bearer of Strength
To the weary-mum of 3 including
Her newly delivered baby.

She just needed
Love to pick her up,
And help her see,
'Now I can bathe the children,
While I have someone
To watch the others'.

'I can have a bath myself while
The children are cared for.'
'I can face the feeding, with
Paracetemol to dull the pain..
I can rejoice in His Name- and live again'.

And so it was – and I just 'was'-
I saw her grow in Strength, Courage
And efficient care for the children
And herself, while I sat on the floor,
Reading or playing with God's Treasures
Who climbed or sat on me,
Listening to me read.

It happened on other occasions with that very God-fearing, faithful Nigerian woman, ME, when I was simply prompted to 'Go', sometimes with no apparent reason – until I got there, and it was revealed.

At one time I was visiting ME in one ward in the Manor hospital where she was suffering with suspected appendicitis, and downstairs in the Maternity ward was my Ethiopian sister, H, with whom I had shared a Caesarean section birth that morning!! God was enabling me to give His love to these women when they needed loving Strength to help them persevere. They bore the burden; I was just carrier of a Heart of His Love!! And I was blessed!! The Ethiopian family used to say to me, 'Our home is your home'...and they meant it! (Both AA and I found great joy in going to both these homes. I always sensed I was receiving more than giving!!)

What was I to do about women as a wider ministry?
Online Courses:

For a number of years, I had been made aware that my singing in Church was in need of change (though to give God His due there were times when I was the only singer, when it seemed the angels sang through me). In trying to improve, I had had medical examination of my swallowing, a long-term problem, and voice therapy. I was told by the ENT professionals to stop singing for a while during the re-training of my voice and throat muscles; then I took various on-line courses till I realised I needed to give my singing voice 'practice'.

I had been blessed to start a **Singing with Freedom** on-line Course in an attempt to overcome these singing problems. But throughout this I kept receiving emails inviting me to join a **'Business with Freedom' course on the computer** – teaching people how to reach people 'on-line'. After much prayer and with great timidity – I signed up for this focussing on the 'reaching people online' rather than the business aspects...

I started doing it while in Flat 7, the large side-slice of the house. But things were changing again.

On the Move again

The refurbished apartments in the now portioned off part of the house, were being completed, along with the renewed kitchen, and the new side entrance in Flat 7.

I assumed that the current 2nd priest with his family was moving into Flat 7 and did not query a move to the finished flats, still believing that Flat 8 would materialise along with the garden which had blessed me for the past 6 months.

Dear Reader, - do not let fear stop you from asking questions to help you 'find the facts'. But if you do keep going the way others are assuming you should because you do not have will for anything other, – **then still trust that God will turn all to Good, for the sake of those who love and seek to serve Him.**

September 1st 2020

I moved into Flat 5 and needed to get rid of most of my book-binding equipment and many books and bedding.

This was a one-room, first floor 'apartment' with a small shower room and kitchen. I had prayed and prayed about getting rid of stuff and really felt that what I was taking was what God wanted me to take and retain. Habtom (husband of the Ethiopian family) helped me build a storage unit/cum wardrobe in the hallway of the flat – using the principles I had learned with the Priest when helping him build bookshelves in the church over the last 6 years.

In organising sleeping, iconography, computer, and printer spaces, I needed to make sure I had space for the opened chair-bed, with the privacy screen available for AA when she was staying over for services and singing.

The only way I felt capable of living for Christ, was in surrendering to the apparent Will of the Father and waiting for the outcome.

I had no specific 'hope' in the Father's actions, but I was full of hope in God to bring about salvation. It wasn't for me to know 'How' this would happen…!!

7

Obedience in Christ : Resurrection from the Dead

Wednesday 16th September 2020

Last night I was aware of a 'half-heartedness/ deadness' and I invited Christ into this and gave it to the Father. In other words, I owned this 'awareness' and invited Christ and the Holy Spirit (who leads us into all truth) into it to bring it to life. Then I slept.

This morning the 'deadness' was a living depression! With no hope, vigour, or vision in the church, I was simply waiting to die!!

> (I forgave all who had ever neglected my needs and care, asked for forgiveness for myself; and asked for the Lord to guide me in all He had taught me, in order to overcome the lies involved in this 'depression'...) He then gave me the Beatitudes to re-absorb.

'Blessed are the meek for they shall inherit the earth;
Blessed are the poor in Spirit
For theirs is the Kingdom of Heaven;
Blessed are those who suffer for My sake
For great is their reward in Heaven.. Amen Amen
Now go child in MY Name and My Trust in
the Father's Provision through the Holy Spirit. Amen

This was God's blessing for me to get on with and learn from the Business with Freedom Course.

It was a six month course, and there were people from all over the world. I felt totally 'free' in the Holy Spirit to engage with this work and my 'parish' immediately enlarged and I started to pray for these people, particularly the women.

I was learning to think about what my 'business' was and what it might offer people... I learned via the teaching in the course, and trial and error in practice, the technical aspects of online-work: for example - how to make a Facebook page – how to make (and edit) videos, and how to connect them to a Page or send them in emails!!

I made a new Website – with fresh blogs – (the themes springing unbidden)– and learned how to make and offer to the public the courses to re-inforce awareness of, and openness to, God's love, truth and provision.

I discovered my 'courageous' qualities again as I would take the instructions for 'x' (e.g. making a video) and see how this could reach out to people (e.g. on Facebook)– and do it…then need to deal with mistakes and new learning needed!!

I began to live the Life and Truth to give through Christ, and to share the Word of God... but it was largely separated from the Parish – until my previously arranged 'Live Video Event' appointment!!

I had practiced everything carefully with the 'Event' time and day set on the Facebook page!…But on the evening when I should have gone LIVE on Facebook – I could not find an active 'button'!! AA came from my room to the office (as I didn't yet have internet, I had permission to use the office). She used her tech flexibility and got me live – only 15 minutes late! But while I was trying to think what to do and say, she busily texted people to say I was live on Facebook! I was shocked to find familiar faces from the parish, sending comments and encouragement!! I went through what I wanted to offer of Christ's encouragement to come to Him if we are weary and heavy laden…. And told people about the upcoming course of 4 sessions which would address this truth more fully! It seemed to me God took a hand….!

And so my first course of four sessions included two lovely women from the parish, and RA from Edinburgh. My 'ministry for women' was launched…. with the prayers of the saints and the blessing of the Archbishop, and the grace I was given to risk the unknown!! Subsequently this course was repeated another three times – and was 'approved' by B Raphael.

Christmas 2020

As there was no base to provide Christmas for others, AA and I were invited to the Ethiopian family's delightful little house that they had been given in 2019. What a relief for them to be freed from the burdens of the political Asylum trail. The Lord blessed us – and I handed over all the 'Christmas tablecloth, napkins and aprons' that we had marked Christmas with for the last six years.. We ate a very varied menu - all with love.

On-going Training – Grace out of suffering

There were other blessings that came from the Business with Freedom course that related to the people doing it. Members of the course were encouraged to share with others their successes and questions on the Business with Freedom Facebook page. One woman had posted the testimonial someone had given her, - and I found myself commenting to myself, 'She's doing God's work'!! So I messaged her and said I would love to talk to her about her suffering, and the work that had risen out of it.

She was actually in Australia, though English, and we arranged a Zoom call. We shared suffering and what had come out of it, for 2 hours!! Towards the end, she asked me if she could offer me something. I prayed and was at Peace, so agreed.

She then referred to something I had said about feeling as if I carried 'death' around with me – and asked if I would accept some EFT (Emotional Freedom Technique) 'tapping'.*

(*EFT is a way of releasing internal blocks that are causing pain, emotional distress or illness, with the cognitive need to 'renew the mind'. It is based on Chinese medicine's understanding of the wholeness of body, soul and spirit – and the effect of being mis-aligned in any area.)

She started the tapping, and I followed suit. As she started speaking about this negative state, and we were tapping - top of the head, then eye brows. Etc I was overcome with a sense of SHAME and burst into tears. When she asked me what was going on, I sensed I could not speak…But kept tapping and opened my eyes then was able to recognise that I was re-experiencing the state of shame and silencing when my stepfather had silenced me in his final abuse.

We continued to the end of my tears and the second round of tapping. What enormous release. And what an intervention by God, through this woman who referred everything to God and was led by His Spirit. She then offered me a scholarship to do her next course starting in about a week. I could never have paid for it. But again, God provided!

I found nothing spiritually disturbing in her course, **The Inner Fitness Course,** which was largely focussed on Chinese medicine understanding of 'wholeness of body and mind and emotions'. She had learned through failure of Western Medicine to provide for her when she lost all power to move or think when training to be a doctor. She eventually had found through Acupuncture treatment the physical, mental, and spiritual help and re-balancing, which led her back to health. She followed this path and did a degree in Chinese medicine. She subsequently learning the stimulation of the meridians in 'tapping' to bring greater healing and restoration of balance in the Inner Being but available to all. The purpose being to heal and unite body and soul, heart and mind aligned with God's gift of life and purpose.

Some other aspects of the course that she had offered me were about recognising the identities we lived with, the beliefs that limit and need to be released and our ways of accepting and facing change. I held it all lightly, in prayer, and realised God was 'extending my boundaries – that He could be with me' (Jabez Prayer). I needed deeper prayer and surrender of blocks of fear, disappointment, and denial. I once heard Fr Thomas Hopkoe talking about his walk with the Cross of Christ, and the fact that we needed to use secular counselling and psychological help as well as Spiritual methods. And indeed, this was what God was providing.

The Lord came to set the prisoners free, and that is what He did in deeper ways through the experience and understanding of this woman' course. Glory to God. Much of it was aimed at freeing the individual to respond to the leading of the Holy Spirit in service and love.

Through this woman's course, I began to face questions to me as a human. I recognised that because of my shame, and sense of powerlessness I did not always listen to 'the facts' because 'fear' blocked my path to obedience to their counsel.. For example, I had read in one of the Church Fathers, that we had to be very careful about habitual 'dying to self' – which could become dying to Self – i.e. dying to Christ and the Holy Spirit within. And I realised that this was what had happened to me on occasions while I was locked into a false sense of 'obedience'. But how was I to get beyond this? I couldn't, but God could!

I had sought to change my behaviour, so I was not provoking anger or displeasure. But I, in Love, needed to respond in new ways. God had been telling me I needed 'cell' time, but I had been afraid to communicate this need, in Christ, to do God's Will. **Dear Reader, I needed to think beyond 'my' boundaries, and see this within the confines of the Mystical Church and a greater reality.**

The next time I was responded to with anger, I was no longer disturbed in my Spirit. I prayed silently, then gently but firmly affirmed the Truth in Christ, then I quietly walked away. I was trusting in God to make a win-win situation. And because of the Holy Spirit in this person, five minutes later I received an apology.

I was sorry it had taken me so long…one-sided prayer alone is not always the whole answer because we need to change our human understanding and behaviour too. Fear and self-interest had held me back. I was guilty.

Dear Reader: take Heart from this 'conclusion' and total change of focus. Through seeking to live for the Love of God that enables us to live in unity, the Holy Spirit provides ways that unite rather than divide. This is the nature of 'win-win'. No 'philosophy' can do the work of the Holy Spirit.

On completion of the Inner Fitness Course, I started another business course **'Project Next'** which had specific help in aspects of the on-line work I had found difficult. Both the two key people were practicing Christians, brought from impoverished and traumatic beginnings, and given grace in the Holy Spirit to find ways to both serve, growing in character and wisdom, and relational Grace, while creating businesses. Through their income they were prompted from the beginning to provide for many charitable outlets.

'I was seeking to keep faithful to the Lord and keeping alert to any 'false gods' that might creep in through the course, while still feeling dis-ease in the flat.'(Journal)

Sunday 14th March 2021

After Eucharist, I was asked to pray about the awareness that this heaviness in my heart was an offence against the Holy Spirit – Come Holy Spirit of Truth. What are the facts?

False gods I have been bound by:

1. False fear of men and authority.

2. Unwillingness to 'stand' in love in Christ.

3. False belief: I couldn't change anything – I had to accept whatever happens…

4. I was still denying God's love and calling on my life because it might 'rock the boat'.

I needed to focus on the beautiful, good and true and the Gifts God had given me.

(Dear Reader-I want to emphasise that if a hand does not serve as a hand with the body, the body is lacking. And so for each one of us. If we are failing to allow God to redeem our souls and enable us to be the Witness for Him that He created us to be, then the WHOLE BODY OF Christ is lacking. This is an awesome responsibility. Oh Lord have mercy on us. This requires us to become 'mature in Christ' obedient to the Father, unto death.)

After further reflection and 'finding the facts' as my first Spiritual Father used to urge me to do, I asked God the question,

'What do I do?'

And after that I messaged another priest who knew me to ask if I could talk to him.

Dear Reader, St Paul teaches us to do ALL things in Love and Christ tells us we cannot overcome the world, except through Him. So ONLY in Christ, through the Holy Spirit of Truth, can we overcome. So dear followers of Christ, take my experience as a gift for you. Pray the prayer of St Paul for the Ephesians, (3:14-19) until you truly are 'strengthened in your inner being, that Christ may dwell in your heart'. And through Him seek the Word of God, and seek the Father's Will, taking every thought and root captive to be transformed through the Holy Spirit.

The priest I texted said he would ring me on Monday, which he did. I explained the situation, and he said 'You need a Spiritual Father – who would you want?'

'Fr Raphael, but he's just been made a Bishop.'

He replied, 'Ask him anyway'. So, I emailed before I went off to take some clothes for Nigeria. I forgot all about it till later when looking for an email. 'I would be delighted', he had replied.

I bowed my knee to God and thanked Him for this blessing. But in God's truth and love in my heart I wanted a win-win situation, and I wanted this change in the Light.

The following day I spoke to the Priest to clarify the situation. I told him – that I needed to move, and 'B Raphael is now my Spiritual Father'. I offered to complete the final three Festal Icons and suggested we meet to decide which prototypes he wanted. I said I was thinking it would possibly be August/September '21 when I would leave.
The Holy Spirit enabled us to stay united, and to meet and choose prototypes and continue to work together in harmony.

I was not able to meet up with B Raphael till April, and then only 5 minutes, after a Liturgy at a city church. But we began to talk on the phone once a fortnight till he had to go to Greece. It was during one of these 'meetings' on-line, that he affirmed the happening and content of my on-line courses and he suggested I record the next one and put it on YouTube..

The Holy Spirit provides for my material needs.
In the midst of these events, I had been 'pushed' by the Holy Spirit, to choose an icon board, and an image of 'The Joy of all Who Sorrow' icon of the Theotokos. While I was waiting for the 3 Festal icon boards to arrive from Greece, the sense of 'need' for this icon continued and I got the chosen image onto the board and the initial underpainting done in 10 days! There are over 30 faces, many of them having visible bodies too! I sensed that the Theotokos wanted to provide for my needs. (Living in this re-furbished apartment had almost doubled my monthly outgoings.)

I then needed to focus on the Festal Icons but included my first 'underpainting' of this Theotokos icon on the agenda, when I visited Aidan. He pointed out a number of improvements in the design so when I visited my friend in Todmorden after Easter, I took this icon with me. Each day I would spend some hours painting – as well as praying, writing, and walking with J, or getting the shopping, she could no longer get without a car. By the end of the stay the completion of the icon was in sight.

Thursday 15th of April 2021

The jaws of Hell
Stand wide open
Ready to pounce
At any pride or self-interest.
But My Father stands
Offering the Cross
To tie me to Him
For all Eternity –
Through Christ my Saviour –
And the Holy Spirit.

It forms an invisible
Wall of faith and trust
And humility,
Between me and
The jaws of hell.

The Truth will
Set me free-
And He lives
Within this shell
Preparing it
To be a Temple
Of the Holy Spirit.

Every day I surrendered to God's timing and Way, surrendering all anxiety about the practical tasks of packing to His Grace.

I continued designing the three Festal icons after the consultation with Aidan. Then with all the outline designs on the 3 boards, I completed the gilding, and got the Pentecost Icon painted in time for **2021 Pentecost.**

Glory to God for the time and Grace, He gave me. I then wrapped up the other icons to take with me.

I had told a friend from the Business with Freedom Course about the 'Joy of All Who Sorrow' icon and Ila wanted to buy it. Wow.... And RA from Edinburgh also wanted it bought for the Edinburgh parish. When it was truly ready Ilana's circumstances had changed and she needed to let it go. But RA made enquiries with the Edinburgh Parish women's group and told the priests about the icon. I was simply trusting in what happened – and finally posted it, with its own plastic cover, when I was told the church was buying it. Truly the Theotokos had provided for my financial needs for moving. Glory to God.

And finally, I started packing all that was to go of the iconography materials.

Comment from 2022

As I recall this time, I remember one Sunday in May, 2021 being drawn to the large Mosaic of the Theotokos, which blessed the 'extended church' used when Covid total lockdown was opened up. (In order to be able to accommodate more people 2 metres apart, the 'back' of the church was moved to more than half way down the hall. The Mosaic was placed as a focal point of the extended church.)

I had so totally surrendered my will I had no thought about how this new life would be manifested. But on this Sunday, I felt called to go to stand, during Matins, in front of this beautiful mosaic of the Theotokos. I sensed her asking me to travel and as I wondered about this – I realised that the June birthdays of my son's family were coming up. With an awareness of the guidance of the Theotokos, I looked in my diary and realised I could not go before the time of the last of these three birthdays - in fact my son's 50th birthday on the 25th. So, I made plans, informed those who needs to know...and prayed about where and when the actual move would be.

Travelling to Scotland

So, I first went up to Scotland for Chris's family's **June birthdays** –only being present for Chris's 50th birthday. AA had helped me find what he wanted on-line, and I was provided with gifts for Jodie, and Kyle. As usual we had a joint celebration- but this year with his birthday the focal point for the first time, Chris actually valued his birthday! Glory to God.

Along with visiting the family I was trying to discern where God wanted me to return to. **Dear Reader,** the sooner you give up trying to go ahead of God, the more peace you will have!!! I thought of and looked into a lot of red herrings re Dundee etc, but nothing concrete so I gave it back to God. God is so patient!!

So back at the flat in Kinston, and always waiting for God's leading, He was giving me courage to daily fill black bags and throw away what I didn't need from Flat 5. I also had strength and courage to start to face the old, abandoned kitchen of Flat 7, which would eventually be one of the rooms for Flat 8. This had never really been cleared because with my exhaustion in packing and moving from Flat 7, goodwill ran out too!

The Movement Forward – taking steppingstones of purpose was crucial.

AA had passed her driving test and was buying a house, so I labelled garden stuff for her to come and claim from the garden shed when she was ready. We also went through the kitchen stuff, and she took what she most needed. I was acting in faith – preparing the way, yet still doing Saturday baptisms with the second priest, and serving on a Sunday as I could. I was waiting for the blessing to step forward.

8th September 2021

I wait for the phone call-
My life given to Christ –
Given to serve in the church-
Yet within, hope breathes and
Surrenders to the Cross -
Waiting resurrection in-
Grace
Truth
And Love.

As time wore on, I knew I was to go to Chris's for his wife's birthday on the 15th September, and I was waiting for B Raphael to bless the search for somewhere to live. He phoned me on Wednesday 8th September, five days before I was to leave. This meant I was able to have a private word in the church with the Priest on Thursday morning and tell him of my specific intentions. I was intending to time my final departure to ensure he was sufficiently recovered after his next shoulder operation. (In fact, it turned out that he was called in for the operation at least two weeks earlier than initially scheduled, so I was able to leave on October 13th.)

I travelled to Glasgow on **Sunday 12th September 2021** having accepted an invitation to stay with Fr A and Brother B at St Gabriel's. I had a blessed Monday, walking with Br B in Glasgow parks, yet in a sedentary gap managed to find a possible Edinburgh flat (Touchstone Mid-Rent Housing) on-line. I was blessed with a Liturgy of the Cross on Tuesday before I travelled north to Chris's in Aviemore.

Aviemore- Flat hunting and Birthday Celebration
I took up the search on arrival and found the contact details of the 'mid-market-rent' Housing Association, Touchstone, and rang about the flat I'd seen. I was told it had gone but given details of the way to find more under Right Move/Touchstone.' I immediately searched and the first flat to appear in the list, had sea views – in Prestonpans, near where I had friends…I emailed – but no application form appeared in return! …so I rang again. 'I've only just put that up!! – the form should be with you now!' said the Touchstone agent. And indeed, it was.

I never saw the details again, but filled in the form, and spoke to the Priest who agreed to send me a recommendation as a Tenant by that evening. I was so grateful. I managed to download all they required except papers which were in Kinston. And by Wednesday morning all had been sent according to instructions.

I put it into God's hands.

Wednesday was Sharon's birthday, and I spent an enjoyable midday to early afternoon on a 'Hairy Coo Tour' – during which we had close encounters with various sizes of Highland cows. It was a lovely day and we both enjoyed it. She said she had never been so blessed with greetings as that year. God indeed blessed her.
On Thursday I had a coffee with my younger grand-daughter, Jodie, and looked on-line at further mid-rent- flats in Edinburgh – just in case, as I had heard nothing.

Friday I drove to Edinburgh and was beginning to wonder what I should do. I was staying with RA and C who were moving into their new flat that day. They had kindly set up a bed for me. Over the weekend I did look at private flats to rent, saw ones in Edinburgh on Gumtree but nothing came of those, then saw a flat with a garden in Musselburgh. Went to look at the outside….. And on Monday morning went to the agent early to make an appointment to view. They could give me an appointment for 11am so I went back to RA's.

Then that **Monday 20th September** at 9.30am, I received an email from Touchstone, saying that if I could get the original letters re. the pensions to them, they would arrange a viewing. I rang them to explain all those things were in Kinston…
'No problem 'she said, 'I can't give you a viewing till next Tuesday'.
My heart sank! 'But by next Tuesday if you are taking others around, it will be gone!' I replied. 'No' she said, 'It's yours!!"

(**Dear Reader**, I rejoiced that I was able to speak the fear that was in my heart! And thus, she put at ease my groundless fear!!)

So, we fixed the time of the viewing on the following Tuesday, 28th September, and I travelled back south on the 21st, trusting in this word and in this provision of God.

When I went to look at the position of 258 High Street, Prestonpans as I drove south, planning to go via Nottingham, the sea soothed my soul, despite still not having any clear notion of the flat I was going to be given. Even the Touchstone agent, who I spoke to, did not know the layout of the flat. Surprises!!

I had given notice on Flat 5 whilst in Edinburgh, and the date for moving was finally fixed for the 13th October to meet other people's needs as well as mine. I sent all the pension papers requested to Touchstone.

When I went to view the Prestonpans flat on the 28th September, all the dates for moving were at least temporarily fixed, but I was assured that this was sufficient time for all the paperwork for the tenancy. I was pleasantly surprised that the flat had all 'white goods, and floor covering' as I had seen that this was not always so. I drove back to Kinston on Wednesday..29th, September, and started the serious business of packing.

AA came most weekends to help me and to come with me to visit our 'families' and Godchildren. Gradually I built up the bags on the landing outside my flat – then downstairs in the hall in a space that did not impede others. It did seem a lot of stuff, but I was no longer ashamed of it. I had surrendered all of it to God, and I had peace in my heart as I said YES to His grace and purposes.

Until the very last two days, we kept the chair-bed available for AA. I was very blessed by her help and presence.

Witness – My Last Sunday in Kinston

I keep my eyes on You my Lord,
Yet let me honour the Love You
Have given me for these Your people.

So as the time for leaving approached..
Week by week, I let it be known
I would love to say Goodbye to 'You'
On Sunday 10th October after Liturgy.

So who-ever I knew how to get hold of-
Especially those who found it hard
To arrive on a Sunday morning –
I simply informed and invited them.

But I did not expect what others
planned -
Love poured out- and prayers –

In the church, the Priest pointing out, with his special torch, the Icons gifted through me for the church, Glory to God;

Then into the hall and
The appreciations of the Second Priest
For the Grace I had been given
To provide in many dimensions of service -
– and a blessing from the Priest.

I found I was given a space to Witness
With words, of gratitude and humility,
To Him who gave me grace to stand,
Through ready prayer and surrender,
Allowing the Holy Spirit space to serve in Love
And Perseverance, while seeking the Way.
Amen Lord. To You alone be glory.

So my silence was broken to speak
His Word, His Truth, in Love
And encouragement to all to seek
His Face and Spirit in Grace.

And their insistence on a group photo,
Which arrived by post -and now hangs
In my prayer corner – reminding me
Of the blessings of this place
And those who still need prayer.

The lock-down embargo on shared eating was minimally lifted for all to be provided with some simple finger food, even gluten free sandwiches and cake. I was truly blessed!

And in the last two days, I was still meeting those who could not get to church. Practically I was seeking to clear up all mess in the flat and 'make good' any picture-hook-holes in the walls. Ha and I had to make-good the removal of the storage unit which had served me so well – but now was needed in its new home.

I was blessed to have a last actual tea with Paraskevi, and a coffee with Fr M at Morrisons. He was a one time resident of the House, now having a parish of his own.

With the car ready packed again on Tuesday night Grace held me in Loving Arms and Prayer. And yet as I prayed, I sensed a 'warning' He was giving me, that I would need to 'sink' again and it seemed March of 2022 would be a time of renewal.

As He closed these doors I needed to start to think of future needs.

Future Needs…

I was particularly praying about the tenancy papers of the flat, as there had been delay in starting the process at their end….and papers that needed to be signed by me, had not arrived either as post, or as an email.

Moving on in Faith

ON the Wednesday, all packed,
With final kind farewell from G,
I set off, slightly after the van.
And each scheduled stop,
I checked to see if emails had arrived.

No sign until
Outside the flat,
In the rain.
Glory to God!!
I had to 'sign the papers'
On my small iphone!!
Praying hard,
Unable to truly 'see',
Grace was in action –
From the onset!!

Papers signed,
Key finally released,
After phone call
To Agent for code;
And flat door opened.
I stepped in with mats to
Catch the damp and dirt -.

I marvelled at kitchen units
And flooring with life and colour.
No grey to be seen, except
The clouds reflecting on the sea
Outside the sliding doors to the
balcony.!

Soon the van arrived, was unpacked-
And men fed with fish and chips;
And wanting to return – they left.
I thank God, and surrender
To the gratitude and unutterable
Humility in my heart. Glory to God.

Comment

I had been moved to a new dwelling, for my on-line work, iconography, and prayer under the Wing of St Chad. All the 'work of the parish' which had provided a framework for 7 years of action and service for God were no more except for continued prayer and phone contacts, and the two icons waiting completion. 'In God alone I put my trust'.
I was spiritually warned I must not volunteer for anything. And thus, I needed to dig deep and keep listening as He leads me forward in new ways, in His Love for the greater glory of God.

PS DEAR READER

I have often thought that our Spiritual Journey through Life, is a little like one of those video adventure games. As we journey, we meet different characters, trials, enemies, have opportunities to pick up 'gifts' which we then need to choose to use in a subsequent adventure or trial in order to overcome. But always we are choosing to move onwards to a greater goal, while serving and growing in new dimensions, as we journey. And we are being conformed, in our case, to the Life, Cross and Resurrection of Christ in Faith, Hope and Love. Have you an awareness of your 'adventure in Love and for Love'?

You have completed reading the book, and hopefully you have been encouraged to seek, knock and ask for yourself in your Life and Faith. I truly believe that if you give yourself – even 10 minutes 'listening' time a day after prayer - God will build, guide, heal, purify and clarify your life in Christ.

Clarify to yourself the nature of your obedience…who are you looking to? Is God blessing this? Step by step you will be led into 'service' which will challenge boundaries you had made, and only through the Holy Spirit will Love extend and Bless that continued growth. Good Strength and courage dear soul to make the Jabez Prayer, your own,

Lord bless me! Extend my boundaries, that You may be with me, that I may cause no hurt to anyone, or myself. (I Chronicles 4:9-10)

Amen

PPS
You might be interest in the 3rd Book of the Trilogy –"He Heals the Broken-Hearted" called

"Children of God: Conformed to the Life-Giving Cross in Joy and Hope for Eternal Life"

If you send me your email: with the book title as the subject, to **marinax7@btinternet.com**

I'll add you to the mailing list for details when it comes out.

But that is not due out till Easter 2023! If you would like to talk about your journey, or need encouragement to walk in faith, there are various ways you can grow in Grace to 'extend your boundaries'. Either send me your email or go to this link to:

https://linktr.ee/h.marina Or Scan the QR code below

Here you will find courses, videos, website, and Facebook pages. May you find encouragement to seek for God's Presence and Work through your life.

Thank you for travelling with me in Faith, Hope and Love,
Marina

Index of Poems

Printed in Great Britain
by Amazon

35767252R00118